Other Books by Theresa Foy DiGeronimo

Preemies: Parenting a Premature Baby One Day
at a Time

Toilet Training Without Tears (with Charles E.
Schaefer, Ph.D.)

AIDS: Trading Fears for Facts

TEACH YOUR CHILD TO BEHAVE

DISCIPLINING WITH LOVE, FROM 2 TO 8 YEARS

Charles E. Schaefer, Ph.D., and Theresa Foy DiGeronimo

Illustrations by Laura Alexander

A PLUME BOOK

PLUME
Published by the Penguin Group
Penguin Books USA Inc., 375 Hudson Street,
New York, New York 10014, U.S.A.
Penguin Books Ltd, 27 Wrights Lane, London W8 5TZ, England
Penguin Books Australia Ltd, Ringwood, Victoria, Australia
Penguin Books Canada Ltd, 2801 John Street,
Markham, Ontario, Canada L3R 1B4
Penguin Books (N.Z.) Ltd, 182-190 Wairau Road,
Auckland 10, New Zealand

Penguin Books Ltd, Registered Offices:
Harmondsworth, Middlesex, England

Published by Plume, an imprint of New American Library, a
division of Penguin Books USA Inc. Previously published in an
NAL Books edition.

First Plume Printing, February, 1991

10 9 8 7 6 5 4

Library of Congress Cataloging-in-Publication Data

Schaefer, Charles E.
    Teach your child to behave : disciplining with love, from two to
eight years / by Charles E. Schaefer and
Theresa Foy DiGeronimo.
        p.   cm.
    Includes bibliographical references.
    ISBN 0-453-00711-2
    ISBN 0-452-26574-6 (pbk.)
    1. Child rearing.   2. Discipline of children.   I. DiGeronimo,
Theresa Foy.   II. Title.
HQ769.S2775   1990
649'.64—dc20   89-12774
                                                                            CIP

Original hardcover design by Leonard Telesca
Printed in the United States of America

To our children, Eric and Karine S., and Matt, Joey, and Colleen D., who have shown us over the years what is practical and realistic in the world of discipline.

ACKNOWLEDGMENTS

We would like to acknowledge all the parents who took the time to answer our survey questions. The results helped us focus this book on the discipline problems most frequently encountered by families today.

We would also like to thank our editor, Alexia Dorszynski, and our agent, Faith Hornby Hamlin, for their relentless support and encouragement.

Contents

Part II Discipline in Action

A Word About Pronouns

Throughout this book children will be referred to as "he." This is done for no other reason than simplicity. The "he or she/his or her" grammatical structures are far too cumbersome to use continually and still maintain a writing style that is straightforward and easy to read. If your child is female, please remember that ALL references to "him" are also meant for your daughter.

TEACH
YOUR CHILD
TO BEHAVE

Introduction

What kind of discipline problems have you faced in the last few days? Temper tantrums? Sibling fights? Bedtime battles? Lying? Talking back? Cursing? How did you attempt to make your child behave? If you discipline like 90 percent of the parents who responded to a parents' survey compiled in preparing this book, you probably used some kind of punishment—scolding, spanking, or loss of privilege. Many parents, even those who want to be fair and sensitive to their children's feelings, end up in daily battles of will and power because they believe that discipline and punishment are one and the same thing.

Although some types of punishment can be effective in making children behave, punishment alone is actually only one part of effective behavior control. Discipline is a collection of methods that can be used to *teach* children appropriate behavior. Rather than thinking of yourself as a drill sergeant barking out commands and cracking a whip, think of yourself as a teacher who wants to guide, encourage, and motivate.

Think back to your child's first year of life. How did you teach him to clap hands, to talk, to walk? Parental intuition told you that you wouldn't help your child learn these skills by yelling, spanking, insulting, or threatening. You probably used positive teaching techniques, like showing him through example, offering encouragement, and giving lots of opportunities to practice. You quite naturally prompted your child to continue trying to master the skills by rewarding even awkward efforts with smiles, hugs, and praise. These natural tendencies toward positive teaching methods prove that you have what it takes to be a good teacher. This book will help you transfer those teaching skills over to your efforts to discipline your growing child.

The application of good discipline techniques is a skill. Like any other skill, you can most easily master it when you know how it works. It's easy to see that if you try to knit a sweater with wool, knitting needles, and high hopes, but without any know-how or guidance, you'd most likely end up with a tangled mess of knots. So it is with teaching your child right from wrong. The inconsistent, hit-and-miss method that so many parents use leaves them with unruly, hard-to-manage children.

This book is your instruction manual. It will explain effective disciplinary strategies that are most appropriate for children ages two through eight. It will help you, guide you, and give you the skills you need to teach your child to behave. Appendix A on page 204 will give you additional information about your child's developmental stages. This will guide you in adapting the information in this book to your child's particular needs.

As you read through the parenting strategies outlined in this book, keep this word of caution in mind: No parent will be able to use all the suggested ideas all the time. Learning how to raise your children in ways that foster self-discipline and a high degree of self-esteem takes time and patience. Don't try to use all of these suggestions starting tomorrow; if you do, you may become frustrated and give up trying. Instead, choose a few ideas and use them as often as you can for a full week. Then, when you feel comfortable with them and they feel like a natural part of your daily interactions with your child, choose a few more to work on. This way you won't feel overwhelmed or incompetent. You'll also have a better chance to experiment and to weed out the parenting skills that don't work for you and to embrace those that do.

USING THIS BOOK

The vast majority of children want to behave, but they need to be taught how to do it. This book will help you teach them through a three-step program of discipline.

- *Step 1: Strengthen the Bonds of Your Parent/Child Relationship*

During the first step of this disciplinary program, you will explore the role that a positive parent/child relationship and good communication skills can play in teaching your child to behave. You will also learn how to strengthen your relationship with your child by using disciplinary tactics that will help you avoid the kind of problems that can put a wedge of misunderstanding between the two of you.

- *Step 2: Set Limits*

During this second step you will learn how to set clear, concise, and consistent rules so that your child will know exactly what's expected of him.

- *Step 3: Enforce Limits*

During the third step of this program you will learn what to do if your child does not follow the rules you set down for him. You will examine a variety of proven techniques, choosing the ones that seem most useful and appropriate for you and your child.

The three-step program of discipline is not a quick-fix program, but it is one that you will use every day for years and that will become a way of child-rearing. If you make a commitment to use these three steps consistently in teaching your child to behave, you will find that you have created a predictable environment where your child feels safe, protected, and in control of himself. You will also be well on your way to nurturing his ability to be a well-adjusted adult.

Part II of this book, "Discipline in Action," describes situations in which some parents find it difficult to discipline their children effectively. For each problem, we've provided remedies.

This section also includes an alphabetical listing of particular behavior problems that parents most frequently face in raising their children. The suggested disciplinary approach to each problem includes a reference guide back to a full discussion of the proper discipline strategy.

Parenting is not an easy job, and unfortunately, the skills to do it well do not always come naturally. *Teach Your Child to Behave* will help you develop the skills you need to discipline your child. Once you learn the techniques of the three-step discipline program, you will have more time, energy, and patience to do the fun things that are also an important part of good parenting.

PART I

The Program

STEP ONE

Strengthen The Bonds of Your Parent/Child Relationship

The first step in laying a solid foundation for a program of discipline is to strengthen your relationship with your child. Studies have shown that children learn best when they feel their parents love, understand, and respect them. But strong family bonds don't just happen; they are developed with a lot of diligence, hard work, and self-sacrifice.

Chapter One will explain some things that you can do to bring you and your child closer together and to establish a positive home environment. As you read through these suggestions, you can choose the ones that seem most appropriate to your "family," be it a traditional nuclear family with a mom, dad, and children; a single parent and children; a mom or dad, a lover, and children; or a weekend visitation type. Whatever form *your* family takes, your children need to know they belong to this unit. The more components of a caring family you can bring into your relationship with your children, the more effective you will find the discipline strategies used in the three-step program of discipline.

Some of the strategies presented in Step One may already be a part of your daily life. Some may easily fit into your present family relationships with a little work, and others may not work for you at all. During this first part of the discipline program, take time to step back and look at the kind of relationships you've developed within your family. What do you do that you're proud of? What areas would you like to improve? Which of the techniques presented in this chapter will help you to do it?

Edward Zigler, professor of psychology at Yale University, has said, "There is a magic that rests in the relationship between a child and a warm, sensitive and knowledgeable adult. It is in the fullness of that relationship that we see the child's path to growth and development." The goal of Step One is to examine some of the facets of this magic relationship that we all seek with our children.

Chapter 1
Taking A Good Look At Yourself

One way to strengthen the bonds within your family is to take a good look at yourself. Your personality and character play an important role in setting the tone of your family relationships, and your attitude has much to do with making your home an enjoyable place to live. To get an idea of how you are influencing the tone of your parent/child relationship right now, answer the following questions. The more often you say yes, the more likely it is that you are already well on your way to building the kind of friendly, supportive home atmosphere that produces happy, obedient children.

- Do you assign a higher priority to the enjoyment of your family and of daily living than to achievement or success?
- Can your general mood be described as happy, agreeable, and pleasant?
- Do you often play with your children with the sole object being mutual fun and delight?
- Are family members friendly to one another?
- Do you make your children feel that their friends are welcome at your home?
- Do you spend more time listening to your children than criticizing them?

- Are any hobbies or arts and crafts projects a joint venture between you and your child?
- Do you and your partner avoid arguing in front of the children?
- Are you confident enough to act like a child at times (playing peekaboo, or having pillow fights)?
- Are you primarily interested in seeing your children happy than perfect?
- Do you and your children enjoy a quiet relaxing time together each day?
- Are your facial expressions generally ones of pleasure and approval?
- Do you smile or laugh a lot while interacting with your children?
- Are you and your children affectionate with each other? (For example, do you kiss and touch?)
- Do you regularly go out alone for your own enjoyment?
- Are you consistently and predictably cheerful?
- Do you enjoy watching your children grow up?
- Do you sometimes bring home surprises and treats for your children?
- Do you know how to use a light, humorous touch to relieve tensions and/or motivate kids?

How did you do? In day-to-day living, it's easy to forget what's important in the long run and get caught up in obligations that can pull you away from your children. As you begin the three-step program of discipline, look for opportunities to adjust your own attitude in ways that will help develop a relationship of mutual love and liking with your child. The following guidelines may help you do that.

ARE YOU FLEXIBLE?

Six-year-old Colleen believes that deep purple is the best color in the world. She wants purple clothes, purple barrettes, purple shoes, purple everything. "Purple is beautiful," she cries when her mom insists that she looks much prettier in pastel colors. Colleen's mom may win the argument because she buys the clothes, but if she ignores Colleen's preferences, she will lose a chance to strengthen their relationship.

The more your child feels that his attitudes and values are similar to yours, the more likely he will be to identify with you and go along with what you ask him to do. You can encourage this view by showing him you want to find areas where you and he think alike, and by getting in the habit of trying to find something in his statements that you agree with. Although Colleen's mom may stop short of painting the walls purple, on the minor issue of clothing color she should strive to be more agreeable.

ARE YOU GENUINELY HONEST?

Children are very intuitive. You may think you're hiding your emotional and/or physical problems from your children and that they are not being affected by what's going on inside of you—but you're wrong. One of the best ways to take care of your children is to take care of yourself. The better adjusted you can become, the more straightforward and honest will be your relationship with your child. Zero in on things that are bothering you and take action to straighten them out.

Honesty also means admitting your mistakes. We all make a lot of mistakes in raising our children. When these mistakes occur within a context of a reasonable, kind, and loving relationship, they can be admitted and quickly corrected with no harm being done. The kind of person you are and the kind of relationship you have with your child is more important than the occasional errors. For example, if you yell at your child for a minor problem when the real reason was your tiredness, irritability, and crankiness, admit that fact to your child. Try saying, "Amy, I got mad and shouted at you before, but I can see now that you didn't do anything that was really that bad. I was feeling tired and out of sorts and I took it out on you. I'm sorry."

The more quickly and frankly you admit your mistakes, the more likely it is that your children will learn to admit their own errors without excuses or deceptions. They will learn to view mistakes as a normal part of living. Also, the quicker you are to honestly admit your mistakes with absolutely no excuses, the more likely it is that your children will see you as more human, and then feel closer to you.

DO YOU HAVE ENOUGH PATIENCE?

Surveys show that parents list patience as the number-one characteristic of a good parent, yet it's a good bet that most parents wish they had more of it.

"The day isn't long enough for me to patiently let Jamie plod along at his own pace," says Marsha. "Even little things like tying his shoes takes so long that I almost always just do it for him." Any parent who has ever been in a hurry to get out the door can sympathize with Marsha, but there has to be some time on some days when a child can be left to try and struggle and try again by himself without his mom or dad acting bored or annoyed.

Like most personal traits, patience can be developed if you work at it. If your child decides to build a bird house, for example, show him how to put it together rather than just doing it yourself. When your child has a story to tell, take the time to listen and concentrate even though you have a million other things to do. If your child can't decide what kind of snack he wants, give him some suggestions and some more time. It takes a considerable amount of time for all children to think, analyze, make decisions, and master new skills. Your patience will support their efforts and cut down on discipline problems that occur when children feel rushed and misunderstood.

Do you have enough patience?

DO YOU SHOW YOUR CHEERFUL SIDE?

Cheerfulness means having fun, smiling, and passing on to your children the sense that you enjoy being their parent. Of course, all parents would like to do this, but in real life it's not always easy to be cheerful. Sometimes in a sincere effort to be a good spouse, employee, and parent, you can get lost in the obligations and responsibilities of your life. Days can pass with little time for cheerfulness, and soon parenting may seem like a grim and joyless endeavor. Knowing that, it will take a conscious effort to show your children, through a cheerful attitude, that you enjoy being their parent.

You can develop a sense of cheerfulness by stopping to look on the bright side of things. This may sound a bit as if you're being asked to play Pollyanna, but it works to lighten daily burdens. Make yourself find at least one good thing in every annoying situation. If your son falls into the brook while he's fishing and gets soaking wet, remind yourself to be glad that it isn't winter, that he won't catch pneumonia, that the water isn't polluted with slime and oil, and that he didn't get hurt. There, doesn't that make an annoying situation a little easier to bear?

You can also foster a sense of cheerfulness by telling yourself positive things like, "Smile, you're doing a good job," and by hanging up notes or cartoons on the mirror or inside the cupboard that will remind you to be more cheerful. You can actively show your cheerfulness by joining in your children's games, by singing out loud, by taking a walk in the spring rain, by taking a ride down the slide, by swinging on the swing, or by just laughing out loud when you're happy. Give cheerfulness a try. You may be surprised how much fun it can be—and how much it strengthens your relationship with your children.

CAN YOU BE COOPERATIVE?

Will your spouse be more inclined to be cooperative if you refuse every time he asks you to do him a favor? Will your coworkers work happily together on a project if you're being bossy or pushy? Of course not. You know that in order to persuade adults to cooperate with you, you have to be cooperative in return. Now think about how you try to get your children to be cooperative. How do you respond to their requests? It is not at all unusual for a typical family to have this kind of dialogues:

"Mikey, would you bring in the newspaper?"
"Okay, Dad."

"Dad, would you help me find a pencil?"
"Mikey, I'm right in the middle of something. There must be one in your room somewhere."

"Mikey, would you put your coat away now?"
"Do I have to?"

"Mom, can I have some juice?"
"Mikey, I can't get it right now. Wait until later."

Listen to the way you respond to your child's requests. Then maybe you won't have to wonder why he doesn't always do what you ask him to do. One recent study has found—not surprisingly—that cooperative parents generally have cooperative children. So the next time your child asks you to help him do something, think twice before you yell back, "I'm too busy."

DO YOUR CHILDREN THINK YOU'RE TRUSTWORTHY?

Building mutual trust between you and your child is an important element in strengthening your relationship. You'll be able to earn your child's trust by being honest and reliable.

Children of all ages want honest answers to their questions. When you tell your son the doctor's needle won't hurt even though you know it will, you deceive your son and lose his trust. Also, if you shield your child from family problems by saying everything is all right, and then he is faced with the loss of a loved one, or a divorce, he will learn not to trust you. It is important to give truthful answers—even to questions about difficult issues such as divorce, sex, and death.

You can also foster your own trustworthiness by never making promises you don't intend to keep. Children tend to equate an adult promise with a solemn pledge. Instead of making a vague promise and then having to go back on it, try being straightforward by saying something like, "I can't promise that I'll have time to take you to the park today, but I'll sure try."

In addition to honesty, you can establish a sense of trust by being reliable in your behaviors and in the way you treat your children. An inconsistent parent allows a behavior at one time and punishes it at another, depending on mood or energy level. If you tell your child that he must clean up his toys every day before he can go out to play, check to see that it's done before he's allowed to go out. If you forget to check one day, or if you do the job yourself because it's faster, it will take longer to teach this lesson and your child will not trust what you say as being serious. But when your child knows what is expected of him and how you will respond, he will feel more secure and trusting, and he will be easier to discipline.

Of course, you cannot always be perfectly honest and consistent in raising your children because you're a human being, not a robot. But you should always try to be honest and reliable in your reactions to your children so they can learn to trust you.

HAVE YOU MADE YOUR KIDS LAUGH TODAY?

In the survey that was distributed in preparation for this book, parents were asked to list the discipline problems they faced during one day and then to explain how they handled them. Not one of the 250 parents surveyed used a humorous approach to handle a behavior problem.

This is not to say that none of those parents have a sense of humor, but rather that they tend to consider discipline as a serious matter that must be addressed sternly. That is not always the case. Humor is a very effective disciplinary technique; it can relieve tensions and conflicts, and yet it is often overlooked when dealing with children.

Give your sense of humor a nudge by considering the following disciplinary situations and finding humorous ways to resolve them:

1. Your daughter refuses to come into the bathroom to get washed up.

Humorous response:_____

_____

2. Your son is disrupting the family dinner hour with his incessant whining.

Humorous response:_____

_____

3. Your visit to the park is over, but your daughter doesn't want to leave.

Humorous response:_____

_____

Before you look here for answers, dig deep down into that place inside of you where you keep all that's funny, and really try to find ways to use humor in each situation. (If that doesn't work, ask yourself how Bill Cosby would handle it.) After you've thought about it for a while, read ahead, but remember: For every funnybone in the world, there are another five humorous responses to these situations. The following aren't "answers"; they're only possibilities.

Situation 1: Get down on your hands and knees. Gallop up to your child crying out, "Here comes the wash-up horse. He runs around town picking up boys and girls who need a ride to the bathroom. Is that you, little girl? Hurry, hop on; I've got a lot of other children to pick up today. That's it. Here we go—off to the bathroom!"

Situation 2: "Listen to how Andy's talking. Let's all talk like that. We'll change our family name to Whiner." For the next few minutes you can whine for more rolls, whine about the day's events, and even whine out a joke or two. (This is fun as long as imitating doesn't turn into ridicule.)

Situation 3: Distract your child with a wild and imaginative story about what life is like for a little girl who refused to go home and lived the rest of her life in the park; make it funny, not scary. Include the details of how the animals all became her friends, how she celebrated her birthday there, about the kind of tree house she built. If you pick your child up and start walking while you're talking, you'll be home before she remembers to complain.

As you strive to develop your own positive attitude toward parenting, look for opportunities to laugh *at* yourself and *with* your children.

Chapter 2
Loving Your Child

In general, parents love their children; this chapter is based on that assumption. The following information will help you strengthen the bonds of this love relationship by challenging you to find new ways to let your child know you love him.

Although you love your child, how well do you know him? If you are curious about your child and learn all you can about his preferences, opinions, beliefs, and experiences, you will find it easier to express your love. The quiz that follows will help you determine how much you already know. After you have completed the form, ask your child for his answers. If your child is too young to answer the questions, use this list as a guide that will help you estimate from you child's behavior how much you really know about your child.

HOW WELL DO YOU KNOW YOUR CHILD?

	Parent's Response	Child's Response
1. What is your child's favorite color?	_____	_____
2. What is your child most afraid of?	_____	_____

3. What is your child's favorite holiday? _____ _____

4. Which teacher (past and present) has your child liked the most? _____ _____

5. What is your child's favorite TV show? _____ _____

6. Who is your child's favorite friend? _____ _____

7. What is your child's favorite food? _____ _____

8. What does your child want to be when he grows up? _____ _____

9. What does your child daydream about the most? _____ _____

10. What does your child worry about the most? _____ _____

11. What was the happiest time in your child's life? _____ _____

12. With Mommy, what is your child's favorite activity? _____ _____

13. With Daddy, what is your child's favorite activity? _____ _____

14. What movie has your child enjoyed the most? _____ _____

15. Who is your child's favorite relative (outside immediate family)? _____ _____

16. What book has your child enjoyed reading the most? _____ _____

17. What is your child's favorite game or toy? _____ _____

18. If your child could change one thing about himself, what would it be? _____ _____

19. What is your child's favorite part of his body? _____ _____

20. What is your child's earliest memory? _____ _____

21. What one thing does your child hate to do the most? _____ _____

22. If your child could have one wish, what would it be? _____ _____

23. What is your child's favorite number from one to ten? _____ _____

24. If your child could change anything about Daddy, what would it be? _____ _____

25. If your child could change anything about Mommy, what would it be? _____ _____

How did you do? If more than half your answers are wrong, you probably need to pay more attention to your child. Getting to know your child is one sure way to create the positive family relationship that's so important to a good program of discipline.

WITHOUT CONDITIONS

You can also build the foundation for good discipline by taking a close look at the kind of love you give to your child. Ideally, this love is unconditional and positive. This kind of love has no strings attached. It is love with no "ifs"—"I'll love you if you do this or don't do that." Unconditional love means that you regard your child as worthwhile and lovable apart from what he does or does not do. It involves recognizing and tolerating your child's faults, accepting his right to be different from you and to hold different values, trying to understand his moods and negative emotions, standing by him when he is in trouble, and being "up" on him when he is "down" on himself.

Make an effort to show your child signs of this special kind of unconditional love by saying things like "I love you just because you're you." Or "You're precious." Or "You're really a special child to me." And remove all threats that use parental love, such as saying, "I won't love you anymore if you continue to do that!" Your children need to feel that your unwavering love is one solid, dependable source of security in this world of rapid change and confused values. So be careful not to use rejection or withdrawal of love as a punishment for misbehavior. No matter how angry you are at your child's actions, he should feel secure in your basic love and acceptance.

You should avoid love that is based on merit ("I'll love you because of what you have done") or expectations ("I'll love you because you have fulfilled my expectations, because you do your duty, because you are like me"). This kind of love is given as a reward for good behavior. But when a child feels loved because he thinks he has earned it, there is always doubt and insecurity that the love will disappear one day because he may do something to displease his parent.

A story of love that was not experienced as unconditional was carried in the newspapers a few years ago. Amy, fifteen, had always gotten straight As in school, and her parents were extremely upset when she got a B on her report card. "If I fail in what I do," Amy told her parents, "I fail in what I am." This message was part of Amy's suicide note. Don't ever let your child think that the degree of your love for him depends on the degree of his obedience and performance.

WITH AFFECTION

As odd as it may sound, many parents love their children, yet their children don't feel loved. This happens because the parents can't openly communicate their love. It's important to show your affection by expressing your feelings of love and liking for your child. You can do this either verbally, by using terms of endearment, or nonverbally, through smiles, positive facial expressions, and touching. Your signs of affection tell your child that you not only *love* him but that you *like* him as well.

Do your children know you love them? Ask yourself these questions:

- Are you absolutely crazy about each of your children?
- Do you smile and joke around a lot with each child?
- Do you frequently tell your children how much you like and love them?
- Do you call each child by a special pet name?
- Do you hug, touch, and kiss your children often?
- Do you praise them more often than criticize them?
- Do you share confidences and mutual expressions of tender warmth?
- Do you ever take home surprise gifts for your children?
- Do you give them loving greetings and good-byes?
- At bedtime, do you reassure your child of your love?
- Do you express positive comments (praise and encouragement) to your child at least three times more often than you express negative ones (criticism and disapproval)?
- Are you consistent in the way you show affection, rather than showering them with kisses one minute and turning aloof and cold the next?

When you can honestly say that you do most of these things on a regular basis, then you'll know that your child knows you love him.

WITH COMFORT

One of the things that adults expect from the people they love is comfort. When you hurt, mentally or physically, you want to know that it's safe to go to your loved one to cry and to be held and consoled. Although the things that hurt your children are different from the things that hurt you, your children still need to know that their hurt, pain, sadness, tears, and disappointments can be openly and immediately shared with you.

Even if their pain seems insignificant to you, don't minimize the event ("It's nothing to get upset about"), or express shame ("You're acting like a baby"), or punish ("Go to your room if you want to cry"), or threaten ("If you don't cheer up, I'll really give you something to cry about").

When your child comes to you for comfort, take time to show him your love by encouraging him to talk about his hurt; sometimes a problem shared is a problem halved. And when you give comfort, don't let your child feel that his need for comfort is a sign of weakness. When Kenny came home from school crying because the other kids were making fun of him, his mom didn't take this as an opportunity to teach him how to be a "brave little man." She sheltered him with her arms, and consoled him by holding him on her lap; she told him how sorry she was and encouraged him to cry it out. Let your child be emotionally dependent on you until he regains his composure and strength. Don't emphasize self-reliance so much that your children feel ashamed and guilty whenever they long to become dependent and rely on you for support.

Some parents mistakenly think that they will help their child build character by letting them work out the hurt by themselves, by not babying them. Actually, the opposite is true. By giving your child comfort when he needs it, you're teaching him that he is a worthwhile person that people care about. This will help build his sense of self-esteem and confidence.

The noted psychologist William James once remarked that the major problem in life is the fact that one cannot feel another's toothache. A sense of empathy offers us the nearest thing to the actual toothache. Sometimes you might think that you can help your child get over a hurt with short responses like "Don't worry about it," or "You'll get over it," or "It doesn't really hurt." But in truth, when a child feels that you understand how he feels inside, he is comforted and is then better able to get over the hurt.

You can give comfort with empathy by telling your child that you understand his feelings and then by giving those feelings a name. Tell him, "No wonder you were frightened," or "That must have come as a real shock," or "If it happened to me I would feel just as upset." Then tell your child about the time when you were upset by the same kind of situation. Let him know, for example, that when you were a child, the other kids on the block made a pact not to play with you and they all hid whenever you came outside. You don't have to pass judgment or decide what's good or bad. Just let your child know that you can understand what he is feeling.

WITH QUALITY TIME

If you really want to raise a competent and well-adjusted child—spend time with him. A national survey of school-age children conducted in 1976 under the auspices of the Foundation for Child Development found that nearly half the children surveyed wished that their fathers would spend more time with them and more than a third wished that their mothers would spend more time with them. This study supports my belief that there is nothing you can give your children that will make them feel happier or more important than your time and undivided attention.

Most likely, you spend some time every day in the company of your children. But how much of that time is spent actually enjoying the pleasure of their company? Keep track, over the next few days, of how often you give your child your undivided attention while you both enjoy a shared activity, and then how often your attention is distracted away from your child while you do something else like cleaning, cooking, reading, or TV watching. You may be surprised to see how very little of your time is given solely to your child.

Make yourself a promise to set aside "quality time"

Quality time

with each of your children every day. This should be
time alone together without distractions or interruption
when you play together or just talk to each other for at
least five or ten minutes. Also, each child should have

his own weekly quality time—of at least one-half to two hours—and this time should be cancelled only under extremely unusual circumstances.

The rules for quality time are simple: No criticizing, lecturing, or trying to get your child to do something. Initiate the interaction so your child feels you really want to spend time with him, and you and he should actively try to think of activities you will enjoy. This doesn't mean you have to give up the things you planned to do; ask your child to help you make the holiday cookies, or plant the vegetable seeds, or clean out the attic. This kind of activity can give you unhurried time to really get to know your child.

Studies have shown that merely being with a person while he is enjoying himself increases that person's liking for you. As quality time intensifies your relationship with your child, it will also lessen the need for intensive disciplinary strategies.

AS AN INDIVIDUAL

Once your child enters school, there is considerable pressure to conform to the group. Teachers need everyone in the class to follow along with the group activities, and children develop a desire to fit in with the crowd and be "like everyone else." The job of instilling in your child a sense of individuality, then, falls to you. One of your prime tasks as a parent is to see your child and act toward him as someone who is unique, different, and separate from all others.

When you take the time to get to know your child as an individual, you give him a sign that you care. In addition to doing this during your weekly "quality time" periods, you can also watch and listen to your child carefully whenever you're around him to find out what he is really like. Be attentive and observant; you will get to know his temperament, abilities, traits, fears, hopes, and dreams. Encourage your child to pursue his unique interests, talents, and goals, even if they differ from yours.

When your child begins to spend more time at his friends' homes, or joins a youth group like the Scouts, boys/girls clubs or YM/YWCA, he may start to question the way you do things. Kevin, for example, learned from his group leader that recycling was one way to help keep the world clean. Kevin's parents had never participated in the local recycling drives, and they were taken aback when Kevin criticized them for throwing away glass, aluminum, and newspapers. "Listen to him," Kevin's dad laughed. "A pip-squeak environmentalist. Kevin, you tell your troop leader that it's none of his business what I do with my garbage. And I don't want any back talk from you." If Kevin has a stubborn personality, he may persist and argue his point. If he is more submissive, he'll leave the room feeling confused and angry. Either way, Kevin's right to express opinions, work for things he believes are important, and grow into an individual who is separate from his parents has been ignored.

It is your respect for your child's right to be different from you that will foster his sense of individuality and give him a positive self-concept. Allow him to speak up at home, to express a differing opinion, and to question your position on issues. It's this kind of letting go that will actually strengthen the bonds between you.

AS A FAMILY MEMBER

While children need to learn that they are unique and individual, they also need to feel part of a larger unit. They need to feel the security of mutual acceptance, protection, enjoyment, support, and consideration. You can offer these things to your child by squeezing into your schedule time for shared *family* activities. You probably have already established family traditions in celebration of birthdays and major holidays, but you don't have to wait for these holidays to foster family spirit. Make some time now for family projects like designing a family coat of arms or a family flag. Or try to schedule dinner so everyone can be there. Or perhaps you can create a half-hour family game time after dinner. Don't let family members get into the habit of going off in different directions. Go for walks together, play musical instruments together, go to the zoo, museums, or sporting events. Keep the family spirit by deliberately making time each week to do something together.

The more time a young child spends in the company of his family, the more readily he will take on their customs, beliefs, and morals. In today's world, where TV, radio, and front-page news stories expose children to conflicting value systems, it's important that they can look to their family for what is right and good.

You can teach your children values that will promote family feelings of cooperation, friendliness, sharing, and loyalty by repeatedly making comments like: "In this family, we all help each other," or "We're the Andersons, and we don't do things like that," or "I'm really proud to be a member of this family." By appealing to common values, customs, and routines in this way, you can help minimize personal conflicts between you and your child, and give him a family image that affirms his personal worth and identity.

THE WRONG KIND OF LOVE

Although it's true that you can never give your child too much love, the way in which some parents act on their feelings of love can hurt rather than help their relationship with their children. Three common pitfalls in loving children involve excessive sacrifice, smother love, and misdirected love.

Excessive Sacrifice

Tom believes that his role in life is to completely sacrifice himself and his personal pleasure for the sake of his children. He never accepts an invitation unless it includes his kids. He never asks for five minutes to himself; he's always there to do whatever his children want to do, and he denies himself things so he can give more to the kids. In return, Tom expects his children to give him a great deal of love, devotion, and gratitude. Usually, they don't, and so Tom feels cheated.

Are you a parent who believes in the equation: "Parental sacrifice = a child's eternal gratitude"? You are if you've ever tried to make your child feel guilty by reminding him at every opportunity of how much you've done for him, or if you believe that your children are your whole world and you've made your happiness revolve around them. Parents who sacrifice too much find they damage the parent/child relationship by expecting too much in return.

Making sacrifices for children is part of being a parent. But this should be done knowing that children may not return the favor. The enduring bonds between you and your child should be those of unconditional love and affection rather than guilt or indebtedness.

Smother Love

Jackie thought she could show the extent of her love for her children by buying them everything they wanted, by protecting them from all harm, and by insisting that she, rather than friends, teachers or relatives, be the dominant person of influence in their lives. Instead of drawing her children closer to her with this kind of dedication, Jackie pushed them away by trying too hard to be the all-giving, all-caring mother.

Even though your children mean the world to you, try not to place them at the center of your universe. All children need to learn that they can't have everything they want, that they must do certain things whether they want to or not—and that this has nothing to do with how much or how little you love them. Because you love your children, strive to give them a sense of self-discipline by holding back the kind of love that smothers.

Misdirected Love

Sometimes in a zealous effort to give your children the best of everything, you might forget to save some of yourself for your spouse. Although child-rearing does demand a great deal of your time, energy, and commitment, taking these elements away from your partner can actually hurt your children in the long run. Numerous studies verify that troubled marriages tend to produce troubled children. So one of the best ways to give your child a positive home environment is to love your spouse.

If your marriage is presently intact, one of your major long-term goals should be to maintain closeness and warmth in this relationship. Although this book can't fully discuss all the ways to maintain intimacy and friendship in your marriage, the following chart of dos and don'ts will help you clarify the role of your love for your spouse and for your children.

Learning how to love your child is one way to strengthen the bonds of your parent/child relationship. The challenge in doing this is to avoid the extremes of too much and too little. The philosopher Schopenhauer once told this fable to illustrate the problem:

> One wintry day, a couple of chilled porcupines huddled together for warmth. They found that they pricked each other with their quills, moved apart and were again cold. After much experimentation, the porcupines found the distance at which they gave each other some warmth without too much sting.

Experiment with your child to find that place where you are close enough to give emotional support and warmth, but not so close that you hurt each other.

LOVING YOUR SPOUSE

DO look to your spouse, rather than your children, to comfort you when you are troubled.

DO confide in your spouse about your dreams and wishes.

DO keep your marriage strong by doing thoughtful, romantic things for each other.

DO realize you are entitled to marital fulfillment even if it means doing a bit less for and with your children.

DO insist on marital privacy and forbid your children to invade it.

DO openly express your affection for your spouse by words and actions. Let your children see the warmth in your relationship.

DO treat your spouse as you did just before your marriage.

DO share many interests with your spouse, since this has a bonding effect.

DON'T expect your children to be your main source of comfort and care as you grow older.

DON'T be afraid to leave your children with a qualified baby-sitter.

DON't depend on your children to provide the main source of your happiness.

Chapter 3
Learning to Communicate

Specifically, communication is any behavior, verbal or nonverbal, that carries a message to another person, but in your relationship with your child, communication is also more. It's sharing, and it's the opening up of the two of you to each other. To communicate with your children, you need to express your own ideas and feelings to them, as well as listen to and understand their thoughts and feelings. Sometimes in our hurried world, one day slides almost unnoticed into the next, and opportunities to communicate openly pass unnoticed. As you work to strengthen the bonds of your parent/child relationship, this chapter will help you acquire the skills of understanding children who may not be very good at explaining, and of explaining things to children who may not be very adept at listening and understanding.

HOW TO LISTEN

A complaint that family members commonly make of one another is, "No one really listens to me." Children in particular often feel this way because most communication in the home is a one-way street—from parent to child. In fact, one study has found that many parents spend less than twenty-one minutes a week really listening to their children.

Take a look at the following questions. Your answers will help you decide if you know how to really listen when your children speak.

- Do you make sure to give your child your undivided attention when you listen?
- Do you find yourself anxious to interrupt your child or to find an opening to start talking?
- Do you tend to monopolize the conversation by lecturing, preaching, reassuring, or do you maintain a real dialogue with your children?
- Do you not only have frequent talks with your children, but in-depth talks in which you share feelings, beliefs, conflicts, doubts, values, and dreams?

Even the best of parents have some trouble doing all of these things. The following guidelines will help you improve your listening skills.

Be Available

Being available to listen to your child is, obviously, the most vital aspect of being a good listener. During times of crisis, trauma, or disappointment, for example, your children need you to be available to listen and supply whatever comfort or support they need. Your children also need to feel that you are readily available to share their good news and joyful experiences.

Most parents make an effort to be available to their children during times of extreme sorrow or joy, but you should also try to set aside routine time each day to really listen. If there's a time that your child usually seems especially talkative (during breakfast, after school, before bed), make that your listening time. Or tell your child you want to set aside a special time each day so the two of you can talk. Ask him when he would like that time to be and schedule it right on your calendar. Let him know that even though you're busy, you're working, or you have other obligations besides him, what he has to say is important to you, and you will make time to listen.

Give Undivided Attention

Some children can talk all day with or without an attentive audience. They'll follow their parents around and jabber incessantly until the sound of their voices are no more than a dull drone off in the background. Most parents can't give their children complete and undivided attention all the time, but when you want to really listen to your child, cut out all other distractions. Don't try to iron, cook, or watch TV; select a quiet spot and an unhurried time, and listen.

When you're listening to your child, you should pay attention not only to his words, but also to his actions. Studies have found that when we talk, about 90 percent of our meaning is transmitted by nonverbal signals such as tone of voice and facial expressions. So a shrug, a nervous laugh, gestures, tone of voice, facial expressions, and body positions contain important messages that we need to decode accurately by listening with a "third ear." A child who is feeling depressed, for example, will tend to avoid eye contact, be "down in the mouth," and show a lack of energy at the same time that he tells you, "I'm not upset."

Be particularly sensitive to the absence of usual nonverbal behavior since this will often give clues to a child's inner feelings. An obvious example is when a child does not eat, sleep, play, or concentrate as well as usual. A more subtle example can be something as simple as not giving the customary good-night kiss or welcome-home smile. Actions speak louder than words; remember to "listen" to them.

You can also show your child that you want to listen and that he is being heard by effectively using your own body position. Your body language should include some of these elements:

Eye contact. Be sure to initiate and maintain eye contact with your child. This tells your child that you are interested in what he is saying and provides you with a chance to watch his body language.

Body posture. Your body position can communicate to your child that you are interested in what he has to say. An upright seated position with your upper body leaning slightly forward is generally considered best to convey a desire to listen. Keep your arms open to signal a receptive attitude; arms folded across the chest and legs tightly crossed indicate an attitude of defensiveness.

Comfortable distance. How close should you sit to a child when you want to have a personal conversation? Studies suggest that most people are comfortable about two to three feet away from the other person. Test for yourself where you and your child are most comfortable. But remember, sitting too close can be threatening, and sitting too far away can seem uninterested.

Facial expression. When your facial expression is alert and animated you will find children more willing to talk with you. Try to vary your expressions to match the topics of conversations. This way you will avoid unknowingly using a fixed expression that might convey boredom or lack of interest.

Give Undivided Attention

Situation 1: Your child runs through the front door. She's laughing, jumping, and yelling out good news.

A Common Response
Parent: "Cathy, what is it? Come into the kitchen where I'm washing the dishes and tell me all about it." (Mom continues to wash dishes, and Cathy continues jumping around and yelling out her news.)

A Better Response
Parent: "Cathy, what is it?" (Mom dries her hands, goes to Cathy, sits down next to her, and listens to every word of the good news.)

Situation 2: Your child comes home from school and does not say hello as usual. He slams the door shut behind him.

A Common Response
Parent: "I've told you not to slam that door. Now go back and shut it properly."

A Better Response
Parent: "Did something happen in school today?"

> Child: "No."
> Parent: "Well, the way you're acting tells me something different. If there is anything you would like to talk about later, I'm here and would be glad to listen."

Ask Questions Carefully

The Greek philosopher Socrates is known for his ability to draw wisdom out of people by asking them questions. Questions are especially useful to you as a listener when you want to gather information about a certain topic, focus on a particular idea, or help your child consider a point. Open-ended questions that begin with "what," "where," "when," or "how," are often useful when you want to help your child explore a particular subject. Examples include: "What are some of the things you like about your teacher?" and "When do you feel that way?"

It is usually best to avoid starting a conversation by asking questions that begin with words like "are," "is," "do," or "why." These are called closed-end questions. The first three words ask for a specific fact and tend to elicit yes or no answers. "Why" questions are sometimes very difficult for children, since they often do not recognize the underlying motives for their actions. As a result, the child may feel defensive and avoid further discussion of the subject. Instead of asking "why" questions, such as "Why are you angry?" ask "what" questions, such as "What makes you angry?" The "what" question requests descriptive information and is less difficult and threatening for a child to answer.

You can gauge how well you're doing with these techniques if your questions encourage your child to talk in greater detail about the topic. If your child tends to clam up or become annoyed after your questions, then you need to examine if you are asking too many "why" or closed-end questions. You should also be sure to avoid the following pitfalls to good questioning:

- "Leading" questions, such as "You would never take something that belonged to Mrs. Jones, would you?" Leading questions only put your words into a child's mouth.
- Long or complicated questions. Your questions should be brief and easy to understand. If a child doesn't understand the question, rephrase it, or approach it from another angle. Don't become annoyed and just repeat the question in a louder tone of voice. Each question should contain only a single thought. Avoid questions like "Why are you crying and who started it?" Such queries lump several issues together.
- Negative questions, like "Why do you look so guilty?" This kind of question is used to snoop, lead, interrogate, or trap a child. Remember that constructive questions are those that are used to understand, clarify, or direct a child's attention to an important area.

Ask Questions Carefully

Situation: Child comes into the house crying.
A Common Response
  Parent: "Stop that crying!"
  Child: "But Billy hit me, and I hate him!"
  Parent: "Why do the two of you always fight? Are you trying to lose a good friend? Is that what you want?"

A Better Response
Parent: "What happened to make you cry?"
  Child: "Billy hit me and he hurt my arm."
  Parent: "Oh?"

Child: "So I kicked him and he went inside and now I have nobody to play with."

Parent: "What do you think you should do?

Child: "I guess I'll go say I'm sorry, and then he'll say he's sorry, and then we can play again."

Parent: "I think that's a good idea."

Repeat Key Ideas

Repeating key ideas back to your child is called paraphrasing. It can be a particularly effective listening technique if you use it in moderation. When you restate in your own words what your child has just said, it returns the thought to him for confirmation of your understanding.

This technique has several advantages. It lets your child know you are making the effort to really understand him. Also, hearing his words rephrased more concisely sharpens a child's meaning and often leads him to expand his discussion of the topic.

An effective paraphrase has four characteristics:

1. It must contain the key thought of the child. Since you cannot repeat back everything a child has just said, you must select the most important and relevant ideas, rather than minor details. Select the repeated themes and strong feelings, since these are clearly very important to the child.
2. Your paraphrase must also be concise; it should contain fewer words than your child's original statement.
3. A paraphrase should be accurate so that your understanding reflects exactly what the child meant to communicate.
4. Key ideas should be repeated in a questioning way: "It sounds like . . ." "I think I hear you saying . . ." "In another words, you . . . Am I right?" By doing this you make it clear that you want your child to verify the accuracy of your understanding.

Some occasions are more appropriate than others for using this technique. Generally, it is most useful with thoughts that are hard for your child to express, either because he does not clearly know what he is trying to express, or because the topic is too emotionally difficult to discuss freely. With experience you'll be able to use paraphrasing appropriately and skillfully.

A variation of paraphrasing is summarizing the main points expressed by your child. Summarizing is most appropriate after a particularly lengthy discussion. A summary should be brief, to the point (include key thoughts and feelings), and it should not contain new or added meanings.

Some pitfalls to avoid when you repeat key ideas back to your child include:

- Paraphrasing when a child is asking you for specific information, advice, or assistance.
- Parroting or repeating back word for word what a child just said; this can become extremely annoying.
- Avoiding negative emotions, such as anger, fear, or anxiety; these emotions tend to make us feel uncomfortable, so we often fail to use paraphrasing to help a child reflect back on these kinds of feelings.
- Overuse, which can make a conversation sound like a broken record. As with all listening techniques, use paraphrasing in moderation.

Sample Dialogues

Situation 1: You give your older child permission to sleep over at her friend's house. This makes your younger child jealous and he yells, "You never let me do anything, and you always let Brenda do whatever she wants!"
A Common Response
Parent: "You know that's not true."
   Child: "Yes, it is."

A Better Response
Parent: "Sometimes you feel that I'm unfair to you. It seems to you that I let your sister do things that you'd like to do. This probably makes you angry."

Situation 2: Your child, age five, is kicking his blocks around the room while he cries, "I hate these blocks. I can't pile them up right."

A Common Response

Parent: "Stop that right now. If you can't play nicely, put the blocks away."

   Child: "Nooooooo!" (followed by more screaming and kicking.)

A Better Response

Parent: "Do you feel angry because you can't build what you want?"

   Child: "Yes. Every time I build them up, they fall down."

   Parent: "Let's see if they'll stay up if I help you. But you'll have to pick up the blocks that you've kicked around."

   Child: "Okay."

Avoid Setting Up Roadblocks

When your child talks to you, you can encourage an honest communication if you remember to use the preceding techniques of showing interest, being available, giving your undivided attention, being patient, learning how to ask questions, and repeating key ideas. At the same time, there are a few listening roadblocks that you should avoid setting up, because they will cut off the kind of communication that is vital in establishing a positive family relationship. These roadblocks include:

- Giving orders
     "Don't talk to me in that tone of voice!"
- Belittling
     "That's silly."
- Being insensitive
     "You'll get over it."
- Name calling
     "Only babies cry."

- Lecturing
    "The reason you feel that way is . . ."
- Evaluating
    "What a terrible thing to do."
- Denying
    "You can't still be mad."
- Giving solutions
    "This is what you have to do about it."

If you use these roadblocks too often when your child talks to you, he'll soon learn not to come to you with things that really matter to him.

HOW TO TALK

Listen to yourself talk to your children during the course of one complete day. You might find that the vast majority of your "conversations" sound like this:

"Come and eat."
"Don't bang your feet against the chair."
"You have to get your face washed."
"Stop teasing your sister."
"Sit still for one minute."

Studies have indicated that most of the times parents speak to young children they admonish, criticize, or order that something be done. It's no wonder that children do not always listen; they don't want to hear all that bad news!

Not all of your talk needs to be directed at your children's behavior. You can also talk with your child about many things that are fun and enjoyable. Make an effort every day to discuss common daily experiences and personal thoughts and feelings.

Keep in mind, however, that talking to children is different than talking to adults. Sometimes to do it correctly you may need to make some changes in your approach and attitude. It's especially helpful if you can

The following list of dos and don'ts should be kept in mind when you're listening to your children. They will help you learn to really listen.

- Hold conversations in private. The best communications between you and your child will occur when others are not around.

- Encourage your children to talk. Give your child praise and appreciation for his efforts to communicate.

- Keep an open mind. Don't hear only what you want to hear or expect to hear. Don't immediately evaluate what your child has said, offering responses like, "That's not a nice thing to say. Don't talk about your teacher that way."

- Listen with respect. Listen to a child as you would to a friend. Be courteous and don't interrupt or dominate the conversation.

- Maintain confidentiality. Show your child that you can keep a secret and respect confidences.

- Keep it brief. Watch your child for cues that it is time to end a conversation. When a child begins to fidget, stare into space, or act silly, he is probably signaling that it is time to end the discussion.

- Make listening a priority. Set aside some time each day, even if it's only five to ten minutes, to spend alone with each of your children. Children need the security of knowing that they have their parents' complete attention every day.

reactivate some of your own childhood experiences and recollections and learn to respect your child as a person with ideas, opinions, and experiences worth listening to.

Give it a try. Many parents are surprised to find that children are very good conversationalists who reveal remarkably astute observations.

The ability to talk to children so they will listen is developed through the use of several components. The first rule in parent/child communication is simple: Be brief. The time to stop talking is before children stop listening. As a rough guide, when describing or explaining you should keep each remark under thirty seconds, and ask your child to comment after each remark. You should feed a little information, get a reaction, and feed in a little more if you are misunderstood.

Young children also need to be spoken to with simple, concrete words rather than with big complex ones in long sentences. Speak slowly (close to the child's rate of speech), and with exaggerated intonation. Studies show that children comprehend better with this approach. If you find that your child does not understand you, quickly rephrase your message in a simpler and more concrete manner.

When talking to children, one specific statement is worth one hundred generalities. If you want your child to do or know something specific—say it. Instead of using abstract words like "love" or "responsibility," describe the concept in concrete, specific terms like, "It's your job to feed the dog when you get up, even if you don't feel like it." The following examples will guide you in turning vague generalities into specific statements.

Vague: "I wish you would eat better."
Specific: "I want you to eat foods that are healthy for you like eggs, cheese, fruit, vegetables, and unsweetened drinks."

Vague: "Lately you seem unfriendly. What's wrong?"
Specific: "Lately you have a frown on your face or you look away when we talk to you."

Vague: "I'll take you to a movie soon."
Specific: "I'll take you to a movie next Saturday night."

Vague: "Don't be a baby."

Specific: "I like you to do what I say and not cry about it."

Vague: "Do you have any hobbies?"
Specific: "What do you like to do after school?"

Get the idea? Now, you try it. The following are examples of vague statements that parents often say. How would you change them to be specific?

1. Vague: "I would like you to behave in the house."
Specific:_____

2. Vague: "I'd like you to try harder today to remember to behave."
Specific:_____

3. Vague: "Please clean up the mess in your room."
Specific:_____

Although there is no one right way to make these statements specific, your answers should sound something like this:

1. "I don't want you to run around the living room. Sit down and play quietly with your puzzle."
2. "Today I'd like you to remember not to hit your sister or throw your toys."
3. "Please pick up the toys that are on the floor in your room and put them in the toy box."

When you talk with your children, it's not always so much what you say as how you say it that conveys your full message. You'll be better able to "talk between the lines" by paying attention to these factors that affect communication:

Volume. Speaking louder than necessary can make children feel intimidated or frightened. Yelling is unpleasant to listen to, so use it infrequently and only when you intend to punish. Speaking too softly, on the other hand, may cause your child to disregard an important message. When you give an order, speak with a firm and strong tone of voice.

Pitch. Avoid speaking in a monotone; change your pitch frequently for interest. Listen to your natural tone of voice. If you tend to speak in a whiny or high pitch, you may have the kind of voice that kids love to make fun of. Practice lowering the pitch of your voice.

Tempo. With young children, adults need to slow down the tempo of their speech to emphasize important topics.

Facial communication. Eye contact is one of the most important ways of communicating interest, firmness, anger, and other emotions. Children are very sensitive to your facial expressions. How you look at them when you talk will largely determine how your message will be received.

Physical distance. Adults in our society generally stand about eighteen to twenty-four inches apart when they converse with each other. They generally stand even closer to children. During times of confrontation or affectionate expression, it is important to stand close to your child.

When you use these elements you'll probably find that your children notice something is better about the way you communicate with them. To enhance this new perception of you as someone who knows what he's talking about, you can further encourage your children to listen when you talk by disclosing some of your inner self. You can do this by revealing your personal needs, weaknesses, dreams, and emotions. Have you ever talked to your child, for example, about what makes you afraid or what makes you particularly happy? A deliberate disclosure of your private thoughts and feelings will often lead to a greater trust and closeness with your child.

Whatever you choose to talk about with your child, don't do it when one of you is hurried, tense, upset, or tired. Find a time when you and your child are both in the mood to talk and you can give your undivided attention. This means you're not busy cooking, watching TV, or writing a shopping list while you're trying to talk. If you have work to do and a message to relate, invite your child to work with you while you talk. Because life is so often hurried and hectic, it may be best to schedule an appointment time to talk with your child. Like all your other appointments, you'll find time to fit it into your day when you raise its level of importance to that of a scheduled event.

These are some of the listening and speaking skills that you should try to use when communicating with your child. Don't be too hard on yourself, however, if you forget to use them all, all the time. There will probably still be conversations in which you only half-listen to your child because you're distracted with something else, and there may still be days when you go on a tirade and yell yourself silly. But if you make an effort to incorporate the communication skills explained in this chapter into your daily family life, the doors of honest communication can be easily opened to help strengthen the bonds of your parent/child relationship.

Chapter 4
What to Do Before
You Say "Don't"

When Johnny began nursery school, his new teacher asked all the children to give their first and last names. The little girl sitting next to Johnny said, "Susie Gold." Another little boy sitting opposite Johnny said, "Timmy Lane." Johnny beamed with pride when it was his turn. He shouted out what he thought must be his full name since his parents said it to him so often: "Johnny Don't!"

This true story illustrates how some parents wear out the meaning of the word "don't" by saying it all day long. To create an effective program of discipline in your home, take a close look at your current methods of discipline to see if they can be altered. Your goals include: preventing discipline problems from developing in the first place; being more tolerant of behaviors that, although annoying, are appropriate to your child's age; consistently giving your child behavior guidelines; and putting more emphasis on teaching your child through your own good example.

This chapter will help you learn how to do these things before you're tempted to yell "Don't."

PREVENTING PROBLEMS

Before you try to change your child's negative behavior, take a minute to see if it wouldn't be easier to

Preventing problems

prevent the problem altogether by changing something in your child's environment.

Sue, for example, was "crazy" by ten o'clock in the morning because three-year-old Sean had already spilled his milk, broken the glass, messed up all the clothes in his dresser drawers, interrupted an important phone conversation, and knocked the plant off the coffee table.

If you, like Sue, sometimes feel like your child is driving you "crazy," check to see if you can change something in his environment that will make it easier for him to behave. You can usually do this by adding something to his environment (such as games, books, safety locks, and gates), subtracting something from his environment (such as fragile decorations, plants, poisons, and knives), or changing the schedule of an activity.

To prevent problems, Sue could have given Sean only a small amount of milk in a plastic cup, thereby subtracting the amount of fluid and the glass container. She could have put child-guard locks on his dresser drawers, subtracting accessibility, or given him the bottom drawer as his very own to care for, thus adding a safe play place. Sue could have avoided the telephone problem by putting off her phone calls until Sean was with his afternoon play group, changing the schedule, or she could have made sure Sean was occupied with something constructive, such as clay, paint, a puzzle, or a game before she made the call. And Sue could have prepared for incoming calls by keeping a few special games, treats, and books near the phone to hold Sean's interest during the time that she couldn't give him her full attention, adding to his environment. Sue could also have put all her plants up on the top shelves of her bookcases, subtracting temptation. In all probability, Sean did not intentionally misbehave. It just happened because he is a child in an adult environment.

As you can see, the key to changing your child's behavior by adjusting his environment is to plan ahead. In the following examples, you would not be giving in to an unruly child by following the suggested preventive tactics; rather, you would be helping him behave in an adult world. None of the suggestions are guaranteed to work every time, but very often they will. This lets you save your big guns for the problems that can't be prevented or avoided.

- Before you pile your kids into the car for a two-hour ride, think of ways to break up the ride, perhaps by stopping for lunch (scheduling), singing songs or playing word games (adding), and leaving the dog at home (subtracting).
- Before you bring your children with you to visit a friend who has no children of her own, but who does have the world's largest and most expensive knick-knack collection, stop and rent a video movie that will keep your kids enthralled for hours (adding), invite her to your house (scheduling), or go alone (subtracting).
- If your child can't concentrate on his homework assignments each night, you might change his homework schedule to a time after school when he may have more energy (scheduling), offer him special snacks to break up the time (adding), and turn off the TV and telephone (subtracting).
- If your two children can't play together without fighting, put them in separate rooms (subtracting), put up a room divider (adding), or send one of them over to a friend's house (scheduling).

Before you scream "No!" and dole out a punishment the next time your child misbehaves, see if you can stop his undesirable actions by adding to or subtracting from his environment, or by rescheduling the activity.

TOLERATING CHILDISH BEHAVIORS

Sometimes the behavior of children, while annoying, must be tolerated without discipline. All parents need to learn how to permit the harmless childishness of children. Some behaviors that you should expect and tolerate are:

- Stepping and playing in mud puddles
- Yelling and shouting during physically active games
- Making the floors messy during play

- Being continually active
- Dirtying their clothes while playing
- Being occasionally careless, forgetful, and tactless

There are other annoying behaviors that should be allowed because of your child's age. Although you can expect your eight-year-old to sit still while he's eating, this same expectation may be unrealistic for your active two-year-old. The information in Appendix A will help you determine which behaviors should be expected and tolerated at the various stages of your child's development.

Tolerating these behaviors doesn't necessarily mean that you approve of them or that you expect them to continue over the long run. It simply means that you recognize that children do childish things and that you don't expect them to act like miniature adults. Once you accept this, you can feel comfortable allowing some "negative" behaviors while you concentrate on changing those that are a threat to your child's safety or cause you and your child particular distress.

Four-year-old Jonathan loves to play with his trucks. During the warm-weather months, he amuses himself for hours by driving his trucks through the outdoor sandbox, over the dirt paths, and through the tunnels he builds with sticks and leaves. When the cold weather forces Jonathan and his trucks inside, the noise of his demolition derbys, screeching wheels, and high-pitched sirens annoy his visiting grandfather. "How can you let him go on like that?" Grandpa asked Jonathan's mother. "Can't you control that noise he's making?" Of course Jonathan's mom could insist that he stop playing noisily with his trucks, but that wasn't one of the things she felt was absolutely necessary to put a limit on. "If that's the worst thing he does today," she told Grandpa, "I'll be a very happy mommy."

CREATING CONSISTENT ROUTINES

Most children thrive on order and regularity. They are happier when they know what to expect from their parents. As you begin the three-step discipline program, try to establish regular routines for conducting daily events such as bedtime, wake-up time, meal times, toilet times, chore times, free-play time, and homework time. This will provide your child with a dependable and predictable environment that feels safe and is free of confusion and uncertainty. This kind of environment puts children at ease, and as their frustration level decreases, so will their disruptive outbursts. (While all children need routine, it is particularly important for hyperactive, impulsive, slow learning, and anxious or fearful children.)

Despite the fact that established routines are an elementary aspect of effective discipline programs, many parents find it difficult to set up and stick to fixed schedules because of personal disorganization, preference for "free living," or fear of becoming too rigid and controlling. Unfortunately, children raised in homes with disorganized or chaotic schedules often find it difficult to adjust to the fixed routines of school, and they act out their frustration through disruptive behavior. Since all children must adjust to routines outside the home, it's in your child's best interest for you to lay the foundation of your discipline program by creating order in your home.

Sally and Joe had a hectic life-style. They ate whenever they had a chance to grab something quick; whoever was the first one up in the morning would wake their six-year-old daughter, Debbie, and whisk her off to school. After school, Debbie went to whichever friends' parent would let her stay until her mom came home from work. Most days there was no time to think about doing homework, and bedtime came whenever Debbie fell asleep in front of the TV.

Over time, Sally and Joe began to notice that Debbie was becoming very destructive. She was breaking toys, ripping apart books, and destroying almost anything she happened to be holding in her hands. The school's child psychologist was asked to evaluate Debbie's behavior after an especially destructive outburst in her classroom. The psychologist suggested to Debbie's parents that she might feel calmer and more secure if they could arrange a consistent daily routine for her. And so they did.

It took a total family effort for everyone to change their busy habits and settle down into a predictable routine. But within a short while they all were able to schedule their work, play, eating, and sleeping time. Sally and Joe also hired a steady after-school baby-sitter who could be counted on to be there every day for Debbie. With a steady baby-sitter and a predictable environment and schedule, Debbie learned that her life was no longer governed by other people's whims and fancies. She felt more in control and better able to discipline her own actions. Her parents had resolved what seemed to be a major discipline problem without once yelling "Don't."

SETTING A GOOD EXAMPLE

Children are the world's greatest mimics. Most of what they know about socially acceptable behavior they have learned through imitating and absorbing the behavior of their parents. Since this is the case, the example you set for your child will be as powerful a teaching tool as any deliberate discipline technique you may use.

The "Do as I say, not as I do" philosophy does not work well with children. Research shows that children are very aware of any discrepancy between what their parents tell them is morally right and the actual behavior exhibited in the home. Do you preach the importance of honesty to your child yet cheat a little on your income taxes? Do you give lectures about the value of being responsible and then fail to keep your promises to your children? Have you set high academic standards for your children but fail to show an intense interest in studying and learning yourself? If you want to teach your child how to behave in our society, you must be careful to avoid contradicting your words with your actions.

You will also make the job of disciplining your children a bit easier if you make an effort to control your own negative attitudes, prejudices, and personal dislikes. If, for example, you have a negative attitude toward your job (be it housekeeping or business management), and continually complain about it, there's a good chance that your children will develop an adverse outlook toward their own school work and household chores. Remember, the best teachers are the ones who are enthusiastic about what they are doing.

You can set positive examples for your children in a number of ways, including facing daily problems with good judgment, common sense, and a willingness to accept the consequences of your actions; maintaining control over your emotions; applying yourself diligently to tasks and taking pride in your work; exhibiting an optimistic outlook on life; finding joy in present activities rather than becoming overly concerned about past deeds or future projects; deepening your close, loving relationships; searching for additional knowledge throughout your lifetime; and endeavoring to become more aware of the ideals and values that give meaning and direction to your life and that you want to pass on to your children.

A great deal of good discipline involves the avoidance of problem situations. If you follow the suggestions presented in this chapter, you will be able to greatly reduce the number of problem behaviors you face each day before you even begin the three-step discipline program. By so doing, you'll have a better view of the persistent and more serious problems that your child needs your help and support to overcome.

Set Limits

Setting limits is a way to make long-standing rules that help your child learn how to behave. These rules give him a framework in which to learn about good and bad, about the consequences of his actions, and about self-control. These rules provide the force that inhibits his unacceptable behaviors so he can become a happy family member, and following them is your child's first step in learning to control antisocial impulses so that he can become a confident and productive member of society.

Take the following quiz. It will give you insight into how you currently use rules to control your child's behavior.

HOW MUCH DO YOU KNOW ABOUT SETTING LIMITS?

Issue	TRUE	FALSE
1. It is reasonable for parents to expect a six-year-old to keep his room clean.	_____	_____
2. An example of an enforceable rule is: "Don't watch any TV until I get home."	_____	_____

3. You can expect your child to mind you when you yell after him as he runs to the brook, "Don't get your feet wet." _____ _____

4. Because children need to learn who is in charge, it's appropriate to enforce a rule with an explanation such as, "Do it because I say so." _____ _____

5. If your spouse is a very strict disciplinarian, you should try to balance out the harsh effect on your child by showing compassion through permissiveness. _____ _____

6. The three-step program of discipline won't work if your spouse refuses to use it also. _____ _____

7. You told your daughter not to walk on the grass. Two minutes later, you see her running across the lawn. This is obviously a simple case of disobedience. _____ _____

8. Rules like, "Don't shout," make it very clear what the child should do to behave properly. _____ _____

9. When you want your child to do something, don't give him a choice like, "You can either wear the red hat or the blue one." This will only confuse him. _____ _____

10. Make sure there is a clear-cut rule against every behavior that is unacceptable to you. _____ _____

These issues will be addressed in detail in the next chapter. Read through that information and then take this test again. You may be surprised by how much you've already learned and by how easy it can be to set limits that can effectively teach your child to behave. (If you can't wait to see how much you already know about setting limits, you'll find the correct answers on page 79 at the end of Chapter Five.)

Chapter 5
Family Rules

The need to set family rules probably isn't a new idea to you. Most likely you already have a lot of rules like "Don't jump on the couch," "Don't spit on your sister," "Don't throw rocks at the windows," "Don't talk back to me." "Don't . . ." "Don't . . ." "Don't . . ." Although sometimes this kind of "don't" rule is necessary, the guidelines on effective limit-setting presented in this chapter will help you reduce drastically the number of times each day you will say "Don't."

All adults have to live within a framework of rules and regulations. The way in which these rules are presented to us often affects the way we feel about them and how well we can follow them. The following example from the "adult world" may help you understand how setting limits in the proper way affects your child's ability to follow them.

• Carol has just accepted a new job and the personnel supervisor has handed her a list of employee guidelines. These inform Carol before she starts working what the company expects from her and what she can expect from the company in return. The company, for example, gives her six paid sick days, one week paid vacation, medical and dental insurance coverage, a holiday bonus if her production quota is met, and a pay raise based on her yearly review. The company, in turn, expects from Carol such things as a given level of productivity, a professional decorum in dress and manner, an agreement to work overtime two days each month, and an acceptable attendance and punctuality record. Carol now knows what is expected of her and what she will get in return. Since all of this is clearly spelled out in advance, Carol feels secure that she will do well in her new job.

• Dan has also started a new job. He was not given any employee guidelines, however. He was simply told to start work on Monday morning. When Dan arrived in the jeans, sweater, and sneakers that he had always worn at his previous job, he was severely reprimanded and sent home to put on a suit. The following week Dan's boss gave him permission to take a day off to attend his brother's out-of-state wedding. Dan was later shocked to see that he was docked a day's pay. No one told him that employees were not paid for days off until they had been with the company for three months. Dan was furious; he felt that he had been treated unfairly and was being "punished" for breaking rules he didn't even know existed. Then on the following Wednesday night, Dan put on his coat to leave work (he was meeting his wife for their anniversary dinner) when his boss told him, "Relax. You're not going anywhere. It's your night to work overtime." Dan finished buttoning his coat and walked out. He didn't want to work for people who hadn't enough respect for their employees to tell them the rules before they broke them.

To do a good job, all people need to know the rules. Like any employee, children, too, need to know what's expected of them and what they can expect when they follow the rules and what will happen when they don't. Limit-setting will give your children these guidelines.

A well-set limit has three characteristics:

1. It gives a simple directive. (The guidelines for setting these directives are given in this chapter.)

2. It includes a reason for the limit. (A full explanation of why reasons are important is on page 64.)
3. It states a consequence that will follow if the limit is ignored. (The kinds of appropriate consequences and ways to enforce them are explained in Step Three on page 80.)

When you finish reading this book, you will be able to set and enforce limits like the following, which includes all three components:

Limit: "Johnny, you can play outside in the backyard, but you can not go in the front yard, or on the sidewalk, or out into the street.
Reason: "In the backyard you are safe from being hit by a car.
Consequence: "If you go out of the backyard, you will have to come into the house and stay in for the rest of the day."

The rest of this chapter will explain how to set limits so they will include all three parts, how to state them so that your child will understand them, and how to be sure the limits you impose are appropriate, reasonable, and enforceable.

MAKE YOUR LIMITS APPROPRIATE AND REASONABLE

The limits you set for your child should give him a sense of security by clearly establishing the framework of your expectations. They should not make him feel overwhelmed by frustration. When you set a limit for your child, make sure that he is physically and developmentally able to do it, and that you are not infringing on his need for rest and relaxation. You cannot expect your three-year-old to watch out responsibly for the safety of his one-year-old sister, nor can you expect a five-year-old to study for two hours after school each day, or an eight-year-old to mow the lawn each week.

You should also be willing to adjust your standards to a realistic level of expectation. Certainly your idea of "clean up your room," will be different than that of your six-year-old. When you set a limit, consider your child's age and his present way of looking at things, and then decide if it's vital that things be done your way. Perhaps, for example, the "clean room" issue is one area where you can reduce the number of daily family battles by accepting a lower standard of cleanliness. Or, if your child is making a lot of noise, or a mess with his toys, stop before you yell, and consider if you might be able to tolerate these things so that you can save your voice for more disruptive behavior problems. Even young children are more likely to comply to rules that they feel are reasonable and are made for their benefit.

MAKE SURE ALL LIMITS ARE ENFORCEABLE

Before setting a limit, be sure you can enforce it consistently. Ask yourself if you will follow through every time the rule is broken and if you will always know when it's broken. Throw out any rule that you cannot enforce 100 percent of the time. If you announce that there is to be no TV watching after school, but you don't get home until 5:30 P.M., you will have a difficult time enforcing that rule. To deal with the daily behavior problems that you can't prevent or ignore, but for which you also can't consistently set enforceable limits (e.g., "Don't yell, jump, run, mess, cry, nag"), you can use techniques like requesting, persuading, or modeling. But when you set a limit, it becomes a rule that can not be broken without an immediate, enforceable consequence.

SET LIMITS IN ADVANCE

Limits can't be used like water that you throw on an already burning fire. They are made to be used as guidelines given to your child in advance so he will know what he can and can't do. Like Dan, the employee who couldn't avoid trouble because he didn't know the rules, your children can't behave if they don't know in advance what you expect of them.

Some limits will become long-standing household rules that your child will know by heart, such as "You can have dessert only if you eat all your supper," or "Bedtime in this house is eight o'clock." But other limits will be set as the need arises—and your child still needs advance warning of his limits. If you are going on a picnic near a running brook, for example, tell your child *before* you get there that he can fish in the brook, but he cannot put his feet in the water because it's too cold to have wet feet. If you're going shopping, tell your child *before* you get into the store that candy and toys are not on your shopping list for today and that you will not be buying any. When you visit relatives for the holidays, tell your children exactly what kind of behavior you expect from them *before* you get there.

Your children will need reminders about these short-term limits because they are new to their "how-to-behave" store of reference. But if you set limits in advance in the ways explained in this chapter, you'll find that your child is better able to follow the rules than if you yell after him as he runs to the brook, "Don't get your feet wet," or if you try to talk him out of a new toy as he stands clutching it at the check-out counter, or if you grab his body in the middle of his stampede, tighten your grip around his arm, clench your teeth, and growl, "Don't run around Aunt Jane's apartment."

Teaching your child to behave requires advance planning.

STATE A REASON

When you tell a child to do something, be sure to state the reason why it must be done. It is easy for parents to fall into the habit of simply telling children to do things without further explanation. "You can't have my scissors" may sound selfish to your child. "My scissors are very sharp and they can hurt you. That's why I can't let you have them" sounds much more reasonable. By taking the time to explain the "why" of something you sound less "bossy" and more logical and reasonable. This will also increase the likelihood that your child will comply with your instructions.

Also, blind obedience will not develop your child's moral or intellectual reasoning abilities. When children understand why a rule is necessary, they are more likely to conform to it of their own accord, without external pressure. Self-discipline is based on understanding the reasonableness of rules. So only in an emergency or when your child obviously knows the reason should you say, "Do it because I say so."

If you calmly and carefully explain why your child should obey a rule but he continues to ask "why?" "why?" "why?", he is no longer looking for a reason—but rather for your attention. Tell him you have explained the rule and there's no need to explain it anymore. Then distract him with another activity and give him your full attention for a few minutes.

BE CONSISTENT

Research indicates that child-rearing is one of the main topics of parental dispute. It's easy to see why this happens, since each parent was raised by different people who used different discipline methods—each believes that his or her own style is the correct one. Unless conflicts are resolved, the child will have a difficult time learning how to behave. Unless you and your spouse, agree on the limits you will set and enforce, you may continue to yell,

Be consistent

argue, debate, cry, and hit, with little long-term effect on your child's negative behaviors.

When parents have different household rules, or when they undermine the other's rules, they confuse their child and place him in an unpredictable environment. This anxiety can itself produce more active misbehaving, and it can also teach a child how to divide and conquer by playing one parent against the other until he gets his own way. Then, too, if the parents argue over the rules, some children blame themselves for causing the conflict and get a good dose of guilt and insecurity even though they may ultimately get their own way.

Tracy told five-year-old Jimmy, that he could not have a new toy when they went to the store to buy his cousin, Kate, a birthday gift. When they were in the store, Jimmy asked for a toy several times, but Tracy firmly reminded him of the rule she had set earlier. Jimmy accepted the finality of his mom's decision without much of a fuss. Seven hours later, when Jimmy's dad arrived home, Jimmy immediately went into his crying and begging routine. "Mommy bought Katie a new toy, but she wouldn't buy me one and I want one. Please Daddy, buy me a toy." Tracy told Bill about the rule she had set before they went shopping: NO TOY, end of discussion. She kissed her husband and son good-bye and went out to run some errands. When Tracy returned two hours later, Jimmy ran to her waving his new toy excitedly. "Look what Daddy bought me! Daddy said I could have it!"

Bill didn't intentionally defy his wife. He simply had had a long day, didn't want to hear Jimmy's crying anymore, and figured it would do no harm to get the boy a toy. But he was wrong; he did do harm. He sabotaged his wife's ability to set limits for their son in the future. He interfered with his son's ability to accept and understand limits. And he hampered his own ability to give Jimmy a sense of security. Since there will be many more nights when Bill doesn't want to hear Jimmy's crying, Jimmy will have many more opportunities to get his own way. As Jimmy gets older, the problems will get bigger. The issues of drugs, alcohol, cigarettes, cars, and sex will give him even more leverage to divide his parents and get what he wants. Jimmy's parents need to join forces now to teach their child how to accept limits.

Sometimes, parents try to balance out each other. If one is very strict, the other may become very permissive in an attempt to show compassion. Unfortunately, many children can't take these two extremes of discipline, average them out, and come up with a middle ground. Instead, they become confused and misbehave more often for both parents.

Make a list of behaviors that you want to set limits on; make another list of those behaviors you will handle with the preventive techniques described in Chapter Four. Then show these lists to your spouse. Sit down and discuss them. Explain your reasoning and listen to his or her response and opinions. If your spouse wants to add others or omit a few, compromise. *None* of the limits will be effective unless you both agree to enforce them consistently. Be sure to explain your new discipline approach to your child's other primary care-givers, so they can support, rather than sabotage, your efforts.

Jack made up the following lists and gave them to his wife, Sue, for her approval. Since Sue spends more time with their son, it was important that she agreed with each limit, and that she and Jack both felt the limits were 100 percent enforceable. (Jack choose the consequences from those suggested in the next chapter.)

If your spouse refuses to go along with this kind of discipline program, don't throw out the whole idea. Continue to set and enforce limits consistently by yourself; do not let yourself be persuaded to fall into old habits of inconsistent parenting. Even if only one parent uses a limit-setting discipline program, the child will learn to respect the limits (at least when the controlling parent is around), and this is better than nothing. It's also possible that when the reluctant parent sees how hard you are working to do a good job at parenting and how well your child is responding, he or she may have a change of heart and join in your efforts.

MAKE THE RULES SIMPLE

When setting limits, the fewer words you use the better. If a limit is too complex, your child will forget what

Tommy's Limits

1. Tommy can eat cookies, but only at snack time after lunch and dinner because then they won't spoil his appetite for meals.

If Tommy doesn't cry or whine for cookies at other times of the day, he will get an extra cookie at snack time. If he does cry for cookies, he will skip the next snack time completely.

2. People are not for biting. Biting hurts. If Tommy bites anyone, he must sit in the Time-Out chair for five minutes.

3. Tantrums will not get anyone's attention in this house;

they are a babyish way to act.

If Tommy throws a tantrum, he will be ignored until he can act like a big boy by sitting still and asking for what he wants in a calm voice.

How We Will Handle Other Problems

Problem: Tommy throws his toys all over the room.

Solution: Make a game out of cleaning up the mess together.

Problem: Tommy jumps on the couch.

Solution: Take Tommy off the couch and divert his attention with a toy he likes to play with.

Problem: Tommy runs in the house and knocks over

plants and knick knacks.

Solution: Put the plants out of Tommy's way. Put knick-knacks in the cupboard.

you wanted him to do. For example: "When you get home from school today I want you to walk the dog, take out the garbage, then take off your shoes, hang up your coat, and clean your room." That's five rules in one sentence! Children are more likely to comprehend an order if you state it concisely and give only one order at a time.

Also, be sure your child understands the rules. Have your child repeat back to you his understanding of the what and why of the proposed rule. This is the only way you can know for sure that he understands it. If a rule is not completely understood, there is little chance it will be followed to your satisfaction. So after giving a new rule, ask your child to restate the rule in his own words. Then correct any misunderstandings or omissions.

BE SPECIFIC

As explained in Chapter Three, try to avoid using phrases that are vague and/or subjective when talking to your child. When setting limits it's especially important to tell a child exactly what is expected of him and when it must be done. If you say, "Your clothes must look nice before you can go out," your expectation of "nice" may not be met. Explain exactly what "look nice" means to you: "Put on the brown pants that don't have a hole in the knee; tuck in your shirt, and put on a belt."

Learn to be specific by including the smallest of details in your instructions. If you say, "Sweep the porch," don't expect the stairs to be included. If you say, "Take out the garbage," don't expect all the waste baskets to be emptied. If you say, "Don't walk on the grass," don't be surprised if your child sees nothing wrong with running on it.

You should also set a definite time-frame whenever possible. Just because you know you mean a job should be done *today* doesn't mean your child will feel the same sense of urgency if you don't specifically say so.

The following examples will give you the idea of how to set specific limits:

Vague: "Be neat."
Specific: "Put all your toys away before bedtime because otherwise you may trip on them if you need to get up during the night."

Vague: "Come home early."
Specific: "Come home by six o'clock because we're going to eat early tonight."

Vague: "Be quiet!"
Specific: "When you close the door keep your hand on the knob and close it quietly. Your father is taking a nap."

Vague: "Take out the trash."
Specific: "The trash has to be emptied into the outside garbage cans every day. This means the baskets in the kitchen, bathroom, and the laundry room must all be emptied. This must be done before you go to bed."

MAKE THE LIMITS IMPERSONAL

Rules should be impersonal so that the conflict your child feels when he doesn't like them is not between him and you, but rather between him and the rule. Whenever you remind your children about the limits, don't begin with "I told you . . .", but rather, "The rule says. . . ." For example, don't say, "I don't want you to hit your sister." Say, "The rule in this family is: No hitting each other, because it hurts."

Impersonal limits work particularly well when you want your child to do something within a particular time-frame. Use an impersonal device such as a timer or alarm clock to set a limit for you. Tell your child well in advance that when the alarm goes off, it's time for bed, or breakfast, or school, or whatever! The more impersonal the limit, the less likely it is that your child will argue with you to change it. So when it's bedtime, point to the clock and say, "The clock says eight o'clock. That's bedtime."

PRESENT RULES POSITIVELY

One goal of disciplinary techniques is to help your child learn what he should be doing. Yet rules most often are set with words that only tell him what *not* to do. Instead of setting limits in negative terms like "Don't shout," say "Talk in a quiet voice." Instead of yelling "Don't throw your blocks," say "Blocks are for playing, not for throwing."

Continual use of "no," "don't," and "stop that" not only sets a negative tone but fails to give your child a clear idea of what it is he is supposed to do. It will take thought and practice for you to get in the habit of saying "do" rather than "don't," but once you get used to it, you'll begin to see that discipline need not always be negative. The chart that follows will give you some examples of how to set limits with positive wording.

When you get in the habit of using positive wording, you'll also find that you'll tend to give acceptable alternatives to the restricted behavior This shows your child what you want him to do, and it keeps him from feeling, "I can't do anything right."

POSITIVE WORDING

Negative: "Don't jump on the couch!"
Positive: "You must sit down if you want to stay on the couch!"

Negative: "If this room isn't picked up, then you can't play outside."
Positive: "When your room is picked up, then you can go outside."

Negative: "If you don't eat your peas, you can't have dessert."
Positive: "When you've eaten all your peas, you can have dessert."

Negative: "Don't run."
Positive: "Walk."

Negative: "Don't drag your coat on the ground."
Positive: "Hold your coat higher so it doesn't drag."

Negative: "Don't color on the table."
Positive: "You can color on this paper, not on the table."

Negative: "No, you can't have a cookie."
Positive: "Yes, you can have a cookie as soon as we have our snack time."

GIVE A VOICE AND A CHOICE

When children have helped create a rule they are more likely to feel some responsibility for it, better understand what is expected, and comply with the rule. They will also feel more control over their own behavior, which is a step toward growing up.

It is also sometimes appropriate to set a limit by giving your child a choice. Since this allows him some freedom in choosing how he will comply with a rule, it tends to reduce opposition. For example, instead of saying, "You must wear a hat today," you might say, "You can either wear the red hat or the blue hat today. Which one do you want?" Instead of saying, "Put some of those cookies back." Say, "You can either put some of the cookies back in the bowl or on my plate, whichever you prefer."

If your child reacts to the choice with a tantrum for the other option of not doing it at all, he's not ready for choices. Go back to setting simple, firm limits. The developmental guidelines in Appendix A will help you decide if your child is ready to be given a voice and a choice.

EXPECT COMPLIANCE

Mark has just about given up trying to make his four-year-old behave, and it shows. When he tells Pauly to do something like, "Put away your bicycle," his tone obviously implies, "I know you won't listen; I know I'll have to do it myself, but I'll ask you anyway." When Pauly yells back, "Okay, Dad," Mark's facial expressions sarcastically tell him, "Yeah, sure. Fat chance you will." Pauly probably doesn't behave because he's picked up on his father's attitude, and he feels he doesn't have to listen because he's not expected to.

There is a tendency for adults to get what they expect from children. If you expect your child to be good and obey reasonable rules, he most likely will do it. If you set only limits that are reasonable and enforceable, that are necessary, and that you intend to follow through on 100 percent of the time, then you should certainly have positive expectations that your child will learn to obey the rule.

USE NONVERBAL CUES TO YOUR ADVANTAGE

Body language plays an important role in determining how your message is received. In Chapter Three you were asked to consider the nonverbal messages you give when you and your child have daily conversations. Body

language is also a consideration when you talk to your
child about the rules he must follow.

Take the following body language quiz to find out if
the way you currently use nonverbal signals is helping
or hindering your child's ability to behave.

Distance
When you give your child instructions, where do you
usually stand?
1) less than 3 feet away
2) 3 to 6 feet away
3) more than 6 feet away
Body Position
When you give your child instructions, how do you
usually position your body?
1) squatting
2) standing
3) stooping
Tone of Voice
When you give your child instructions, is your voice:
1) pleasant?
2) neutral?
3) stern?
Eye Contact
When you give your child instructions, do you:
1) look directly at your child?
2) make sure your child is looking back at you also?
3) look away at other things, like at the job you want
   him to do?

To grade your use of body language, take a look at the
following results of a 1985 study by Hudson and Blane.
These researchers used these same components to rate
how successfully or unsuccessfully 16 mothers were each
able to give 265 commands to their children.

Distance

- Eighty-three commands were successfully followed
  when the parents stood LESS THAN THREE FEET
  away from the children.

- Twenty commands were successfully followed when the parents stood BETWEEN 3 AND 6 FEET away from the children.
- Only 15 commands were successfully followed when the parents stood MORE THAN 6 FEET away from the children.

Parents who stood LESS THAN 3 FEET AWAY from their children were most successful. So the best answer on your test is #1.

Body Position

- Ninety-six commands were successfully followed when the parents SQUATTED while giving the instructions.
- Twelve commands were successfully followed when the parents STOOD while giving the instructions.
- Only five commands were successfully followed when the parents STOOPED while giving the instructions.

Parents who SQUATTED while giving instructions were most successful. So the best answer on your test was #1.

Tone of Voice

- Fifty-four commands were followed successfully when the parents used a PLEASANT tone of voice.
- Forty-six commands were followed successfully when the parents used a NEUTRAL tone of voice.
- Only eighteen commands were followed successfully when the parents used a STERN tone of voice.

Parents who used a PLEASANT tone of voice were most successful. So the best answer on your test is #1.

Eye Contact

The video tapes that were used to record the sessions for this study were not able to assess the total use of eye contact. Therefore reliable numbers are not available.

Based on the results of other studies, however, the best answers on your test is #2.

The results of this study and my own experience show a strong connection between the correct use of nonverbal cues and the probability that a child will obey a rule.

When you set limits, be sure you:

- Are within three feet of your child.
- Squat down to his level and make some kind of physical contact, such as putting your hand on his shoulder or holding both his hands or arms.
- Use a tone of voice that is pleasant yet firm. Make sure your voice is not so weak that it is easily ignored, nor so loud that it seems hostile.
- Look directly into your child's eyes and be sure he is looking back at you when you start to instruct.

USE LIMITS SPARINGLY

In Chapter Four, it was briefly mentioned that saying no to your child all day long will eventually make him turn a deaf ear to the sound of the word. That's why you have to choose a reasonable number of limits to set (you can usually keep a household running smoothly with a maximum of ten limits), insist that these rules be followed *at all times*, and consistently follow through with appropriate consequences if a rule is broken. (See Step Three, page 80, for details about enforcing limits.) This takes a lot of time, energy, and commitment—but it works!

Numerous research reports have found that the parents who have the most trouble teaching their children to behave are those who set no limits on their children's behavior and those who set too many limits. So although it's important for all parents to use limits to control undesirable behaviors and teach children that they must learn to follow the rules of the household, it's also important to be sure that the child isn't being given too many rules to follow or being made to feel like a robot who has

Nonverbal cues

little control over his life. You can find the middle ground between the extremes of being too permissive and too strict by using the three-step program of discipline to strengthen the bonds of your parent/child relationship, to help you set a maximum of ten limits to control your child's negative behaviors, and to enforce those limits with the strategies explained in the next chapter.

ANSWERS

(to the quiz on page 56)

All of the answers are "FALSE." Here's why:

1. A six-year-old has no personal reason to keep his room up to his parent's standard of cleanliness. This kind of rule will seem unreasonable to a child.
2. If you can't be there to personally enforce a rule, you won't be able to consistently enforce it.
3. Children need advance warning of exactly where their limits are; parents also need to set these limits when they have their child's full attention.
4. Children are more likely to conform to a rule if they understand why the rule is necessary.
5. When parents use opposing methods of discipline, most children become confused and misbehave more often for both parents.
6. Even if only one parent uses this program, the child will learn to respect limits (at least when the controlling parent is around), and that's better than nothing.
7. Parents must be specific when they make rules. It's not at all unusual for children to view "running" on the grass as something completely different from "walking" on it.
8. This kind of rule tells a child what NOT to do. The best rules use positive wording and say, "Talk in a quiet voice."
9. Freedom to choose usually reduces opposition.
10. Children should not be given too many rules to follow. It makes them feel like robots who have little control over their own lives.

STEP THREE

Enforce Limits

Does this sound familiar? "DO WHAT YOU'RE TOLD
—OR ELSE!" The "or else!" part of discipline is called
the consequence. All parents use it to make their children behave. It would be nice if children behaved appropriately all the time just because they are supposed to,
but it doesn't work that way. Children, like most adults,
need to know that their actions will be followed by consequences that will either motivate them to do right or
make them avoid doing wrong. The enforcing consequences
explained in this chapter will help you learn how to use
positive motivation as well as negative consequences properly to teach your child to behave.

There are four types of consequences:

Rewards. These are positive consequences that help
motivate your child to do what's right. You might say,
"Do what you're told and you can have a special treat."

Doing nothing. Allowing your child to misbehave without imposing a penalty is sometimes an effective way
to teach your child the natural consequences of his
own actions and can also show him that negative
behavior won't get your attention. "Put your dirty
clothes in the hamper, or you won't have anything
clean to wear," you might say, or "You might as well

do as you're told, because I'm going to ignore your tantrum."

Stating a warning. Warnings are given to remind and prompt children to behave. They are used to give children who are just learning how to behave one more chance to get it right. A warning such as "Stephanie, the rule is no throwing sand at the other children. If you do it again, you will not be allowed to play in the sandbox for the rest of the day" will clearly remind children what is expected of them and exactly what will happen if they misbehave.

Imposing a penalty. Penalties are negative consequences that are unpleasant for your child and help keep him on the right track. To give notice of a penalty, you might say, "Do what you're told or you can't watch TV tonight."

As you read through the next few chapters, you can pick out the kinds of consequences that you are most comfortable using and that are the most appropriate for enforcing the limits you set. Keep in mind, however, that overusing negative consequences (the kind of discipline you probably already use most often) can be harmful both to your child's self-esteem and to your relationship with him.

Children who are disciplined with only negative consequences may learn to behave, but they often do it with a grudge against their parents and with no internal sense of accomplishment. Children who are disciplined with positive reinforcement and the promise of rewards are much more likely to want to do good and often grow up with a greater sense of self-discipline. You will find that the job of enforcing the limits you set for your children will be much easier and more effectively done if you can change your belief that punishment is the only way to enforce these rules. Give the other enforcers a try before you settle back into the habit of dishing out punishment.

Whichever kinds of consequences you choose to use, there are two aspects of enforcement that will always apply: It must be done consistently and it must be done immediately.

You must consistently use the promised consequence every time it is necessary. There is a simple rule of learning that says, "A 100 percent response to five rules is better than a 50 percent response to ten rules." So when you set limits, make sure you are willing to enforce them 100 percent of the time—and then do it.

The previous chapter explained how to specify in advance a consequence when setting up a limit. Do you remember this limit described on page 63?

> Tommy can eat cookies, but only at snack time after lunch and after dinner because then they won't ruin his appetite for his meals. If he doesn't cry or whine to have cookies at other times of the day, he will get an extra cookie at snack time. If he does cry for cookies, he will skip the next snack time completely.

Tommy's parents can only use that limit if they have an extra cookie to give him and if they are determined enough to really make Tommy skip his next snack time. You will not be able to successfully enforce any of the limits you set if your child feels that you don't mean what you say. If you had a friend who always promised you things ("I'll help you clean out your garage next week," "I'll drop by for a visit next Saturday," "I'll bring over my special pasta meal for dinner next Wednesday") but seldom did any of them, you would soon learn not to listen anymore and you would certainly not wait around for her. Well, your child, too, will learn not to abide by the limits you set if you don't consistently come through with the promised consequence.

If there have been times when you've promised things to your child, like a trip to the movies or a swat on the rear end, but you didn't follow through and do it, your child probably remembers. So, as you start the three-step discipline program, give your child time to adjust to the idea that the next time you say "I mean it," you really do. At first he'll probably continue his negative behavior in the belief that, like old times, you'll eventually give in to what he wants, or you'll be too busy or distracted to enforce the consequence (a major reason kids act up more in department stores, when you're on the phone, and when the house is full of company), or you won't really give him a reward anyway. When you set a consequence, be sure you're willing to deliver every time it's due.

You must give the promised consequence immediately. It is important to catch your child in the act or within a second or two of the act; young children won't connect a delayed reinforcement with the initial behavior, so no learning will occur. If Tommy learns to wait until snack time to have his cookie and then his mom tells him she doesn't have any more but she'll buy some at the store later in the day, the power of positive reinforcement is lost. Tomorrow, Tommy will not feel there's a good reason for waiting until snack time for his cookie. If Tommy breaks a rule and his mom tells him, "You're gonna get it when your father gets home," the power of the negative consequence is lost. Tommy may get punished later, but it will have little effect on his desire to obey the rules.

To enforce broken rules immediately takes a lot of energy and determination, but so do most of the things that are worth having, and certainly having a well-behaved child is worth the effort. Wherever you are, whatever you're doing, whoever else is around, promise your child and yourself that you will give him his reward or his penalty within seconds of meeting or breaking the limit. When you do this, your child will quickly learn that you mean business.

Chapter 6
Four Methods of Enforcement

REWARD

Most people have a better attitude toward an unpleasant task and are more likely to follow through to the best of their ability when they believe there is something positive in it for them. Employees who do a job only to avoid being fired or reprimanded do not work as well or with as much vigor and motivation as those who are promised some personal gain like a promotion or a pay raise. In the same way, children respond better to the limits you set on their behavior if they feel there's something in it for them. It's also a basic law of human nature that people tend to repeat acts that bring them pleasure or enjoyment. If behaving brings your child a reward, he is likely to behave more often.

That's the role of rewards—to motivate your child to want to obey his limits and to encourage him to repeat his acts of good behavior. As logical as all this sounds, most parents don't use positive consequences nearly as often as they use negative ones. If a child is told he must put his bike in the garage each night and he does it for five days in a row but forgets on the sixth night, which day do you think he'll get his parents' attention? On the sixth, of course, because most parents are used to a disciplinary approach that stresses the negative.

This kind of discipline approach sets up what has been called the scolding chain. If, for example, a child is playing quietly, no one will say anything to him about his good behavior. Then when he jumps up and starts yelling, he will be scolded and sent back to play quietly. When he is quiet again no one will comment on his good behavior, so he will jump up and yell again, and again he will get attention with a scolding. If his parents learn to take a few seconds to shift the emphasis from what the child does wrong to what he does right ("It's good to see you playing so quietly while your baby sister is sleeping. You're being a very considerate big brother"), they will find it much easier to enforce the rule about quiet play during naptime.

Some parents hesitate to offer rewards to enforce limits because it sounds too much like bribery. A common reaction to the idea of reward is "I'm not going to bribe my kids to do what is right." That's why it's important to state right from the start: *Rewards are not bribes.*

A reward is a compensation for good, meritorious, or desired behaviors; a bribe is a payoff to stop inappropriate behavior. For a reward to be effective, first the appropriate behavior occurs, and then the reward is given. ("Clean up all your toys and then I'll read you a special story.") Bribery reverses this order—the payoff comes before the appropriate behavior. So a bribe is given to stop misbehavior (a child is given twenty-five cents to stay away from his little brother), or to prevent misbehavior from occurring ("I'll give you a cookie now if you promise not to throw a tantrum in the supermarket"), while rewards are things that your child can work for, and earn, and achieve. That's why rewards give your child a sense of accomplishment and self-esteem.

Children, like adults, need incentives to improve their behavior. Adults make frequent use of incentives in their daily interactions. Businesses give bonuses or merit pay for superior performances; police departments offer rewards for information leading to the capture of criminals; the IRS grants tax rebates to those who invest in energy-saving devices, and mail-order companies give premiums to customers who enclose payment with an order. There is no reason to avoid using appropriate rewards to help teach your child how to behave, especially when he is just learning a new skill (like playing alone for a few minutes), or when he is having trouble getting over a difficult hurdle (like putting his BMs in the toilet).

There are two types of rewards: concrete and social. This section will explore the two kinds of positive reinforcers that can be used to help your child obey the limits you set for him.

Concrete Rewards

Concrete rewards are tangible things or privileges, such as food, money, toys, or special activities. The following guidelines will help you use this kind of consequence effectively.

Concrete rewards can be used to encourage good behavior. A mistake that many parents make is to take good behavior for granted and to pay attention to the behaviors they really don't like. When you scold a child, you must pay attention to him; this attention may actually reinforce the misbehavior. The solution here is to give the positive reinforcement (rewards) to support only desired behavior. If your child is playing quietly, for example, go over and praise him for doing so by giving him some attention and an edible treat like popcorn. Try to ignore the times he plays noisily.

You should make concrete rewards dependent on good behavior. This kind of contingent reward is sometimes called "Grandma's Rule." Basically, these rules state that work must come before pleasure. The everyday rewards or pleasant events are made contingent upon the performance of work or unpleasant activities. Examples of this kind of rule include: "Eat your vegetables and then you can have dessert," "You may visit your friend after you take out the trash," and "when you finish cleaning your room, we'll make cookies."

When you give concrete rewards, be specific about why

you are doing it. Don't reward a child for some vague trait such as "being good." Instead, reinforce more specific behaviors such as sharing toys with others, sitting quietly in a restaurant, listening to your directions.

Rewards should be given with regularity in the early stages of the learning process. To establish a behavior in your child, you should reward *all* of his attempts to use that behavior. Once the behavior is firmly established, then you can give the reward less and less frequently until finally you phase it out completely. When a negative behavior is stopped and an alternate good behavior takes its place, there's no longer a need for concrete rewards. If you continue to reward when it's no longer necessary, your child may grow to expect rewards for anything and everything. Children need to learn that some things must be done because they are a necessary part of life. They also need to develop internal sources of self-satisfaction, to realize that things like virtue and success are sources of rewards in themselves.

The best kind of reward is anything your child likes. If your child likes to watch TV, use "Grandma's Rule" and make TV watching in the evening depend on doing homework after school. Or, if your child likes to eat french fries but not meat, you can make an extra portion of french fries the reward for eating a portion of meat.

Whenever possible, you should also try to make the reward relate to the behavior. If, for example, your child is learning to keep his clothes off the floor (in his drawers, or in the hamper), an appropriate reward would be a cartoon T-shirt or football jersey. If he shows that he can play quietly when you ask him, a new "quiet time" toy would be a nice way to reward him. The more you know about your children and their individual interests, likes, and activities, the more skillful you will be in finding effective rewards. So observe what your child likes and how he spends his free time.

Knowledge of child development is also helpful in determining what kinds of rewards to use. For instance, candy has been found to be a more effective reward than praise with four- and five-year-olds. Older children will not be as motivated by food or games, but will work for special privileges and extra money. See Appendix A for more information on child development.

Token Rewards

When you can't immediately give your child his rewards (if it's a trip to the movies, for example), be sure to at least give him an immediate token reward, such as a star or a funny sticker on a progress chart. (See page 89 for a sample progress chart.) This will help him make the connection between his good behavior and a reward. The trip to the movies will be nice, but he may not really understand the connection between something he did last week and this special treat.

For example, Jenny wanted her friend to sleep over, and her parents wanted her to clean up her toys every day. So together they worked out a reward plan by which Jenny could earn the sleepover by picking up all her toys every night just before dinner for six nights in a row. Jenny's progress chart looked like this:

BEHAVIOR	MON.	TUES.	WED.	THURS.	FRI.	SAT.	SUN.
Pick up toys at 5:00 p.m.	☆	☆	☆	☆	☆	☆	

Jenny earned her sleepover, and her mom and dad didn't have to argue with Jenny about cleaning up her toys. Next week Jenny's parents will offer a smaller reward and so on until Jenny is in the habit of cleaning up after herself and no longer needs concrete incentives. See page 89 for a blank Token Reward Progress Chart.

Keep track of how well concrete rewards entice your child to behave. If the reward you're using isn't working, you should either vary the rewards you offer so your child doesn't lose interest in working to gain them, find a more powerful reward, or try for a smaller behavior change. Remember, the first little steps toward self-control deserve concrete rewards that motivate.

Token Reward Progress Chart

BEHAVIOR	MON.	TUES.	WED.	THURS.	FRI.	SAT.	SUN.

Social Rewards

Social rewards are positive consequences that motivate children to behave through the use of praise, recognition, approval, and attention. This kind of positive reinforcement is an important part of Step One in this discipline program because it is a quick, simple way to promote good feelings and help your child feel pleasure and pride in his daily accomplishments.

For example, Joan used a social reward when she looked out the window and saw six-year-old Diane giving the dog a fresh bowl of water, even though it wasn't her job to do that. Although Joan was busy cleaning the kitchen, she took the time to go out and tell Diane that she was very happy to see her taking such good care of the dog. Diane was delighted by her mother's attention and asked if she could do this job every day. Praise alone turned a chore into a privilege.

Social rewards

Social rewards can also be used now in Step Three to help you enforce the limits you set on your child's behavior. For example, when Mike saw four-year-old Kevin playing nicely with his sister, he took the time to comment, "You are being a very good big brother today. I didn't even have to remind you about the rule that says: No yelling at your sister. I'm very proud of you." In this way social rewards alone can encourage your child to repeat good behaviors.

Social rewards can (and should) be tagged onto concrete rewards, as in, "I want you to know that you have made me very happy because you finished your chore of cleaning the playroom without complaining. Now that it's clean, you can invite a friend over to play."

Social rewards have the advantage over concrete ones because the use of material rewards or special privileges needs to be carefully monitored and eventually phased out so that children don't learn to expect a "gift" every time they do what's right. But social rewards can be given whenever appropriate; they never need to be phased out; they can be carried around with you at all times; they don't cost any money, and most children will work very hard to get you to use them. Start practicing this discipline technique today. Use it by itself; use it along with concrete rewards; use it the next time you see your child. Give him a smile and a compliment.

To use praise as a positive reinforcer most effectively, remember: The goal of praise is to show in a clear, objective way that there is cause for your child to feel proud of his work. If you are observant, you will find many opportunities each day to give this kind of positive reinforcement. Try saying things like "That was a very thoughtful thing you did," or "You really know a lot about science," or "You were really patient while I was on the phone."

Praise gives children a needed sense of worth, competence, and confidence. It increases their ability to absorb failure and take risks. Yet despite all the good that praise can do for children, in most homes words of praise and approval are few and far between. Rather than praising, parents tend to blame and punish even though this approach to discipline has been proven to have a minimal effect on long-term behavior. Of course, parents don't do this because they want to be mean and ineffectual; They do it because that's how they were raised and because it has become a bad habit. The information in this book will help you break bad habits that stand between your child and the development of good behavior. How this happens was recently demonstrated at a parenting class when Barbara, the mother of a rambunctious six-year-old, stood up and announced:

"I was shocked! I went home last week from our meeting and decided to use my usual approach to child care for the next day, but I hung a paper on the kitchen cabinet to use as a score card. I put a mark on the paper every time I gave Sara some kind of positive reinforcement like we talked about last week, and I also put a mark each time I scolded her or used some other kind of corrections or punishment. Look at this!" Barbara held up her paper that looked like this:

Rewards	Punishment
I	IIII IIII

"And the one time I said something nice," laughed Barbara, "it was because she did me a personal favor. For the past six years I've thought that I was a good, kind, understanding mom. I can't believe how I've ignored the positive things she does.

"So the next day, I made a real effort to take notice of Sara's good behaviors. I didn't want to overdo it and risk sounding insincere, but there were a lot of times when she really was making an effort to follow a rule or do what I asked her to do. I'm not sure how this will affect the ease of disciplining in the future, but in the past week Sara has been more cooperative, happier, and more visibly proud of herself than I've ever seen her before. It seemed to be much easier this past week for Sara to be good."

Barbara is right. It is easier to follow rules that promise positive attention in return. The following guidelines will help you use social rewards to their fullest advantage.

Be Specific

When praising your children, avoid using vague words like "terrific," "good," or "wonderful." When people make such general evaluations they tend to exaggerate, and so the praise sounds false. (Children are very much aware when they really didn't do that well.)

Zero in on and specifically describe the worthwhile behavior that you want to reinforce. Instead of saying "What a terrific drawing!" you might say "That drawing really gives me a feeling of being at the beach."

Also, be sure to praise observable actions of your child, not the whole child. Rather than praise a child's total personality ("You're a great kid!"), praise his specific behaviors. ("It takes a lot of strength to move that heavy workbench.") Statements that praise in very specific ways are more informative and realistic.

Give Immediately

In general, it is best to give praise immediately, preferably while the child is still in the act. However, it is also sometimes effective to tell your child that you have been thinking about something he did a while ago, and then give a compliment.

Use Indirect Praise

Often it is effective to praise a child indirectly and casually by talking about him at a time when your child can hear it. You can do this at the supper table, or when you're on the telephone, or even when you meet a friend on the street. In this way, there is no implied demand on the child to behave in a certain way—just a statement of fact and respect.

Use Praise in Moderation

Praise is like frosting on a cake—if you use too little it is not enough; if you use too much it is too sweet. Give praise freely when it is due because of effort or achievement, but do not overuse praise by giving it for every little thing a child does.

Don't Mix Praise and Criticism

You can avoid spoiling praise by staying away from comments like the following, which imply criticism:

"You did a good job—at last."

"You played very nicely this afternoon for a change."

"That's good, now why didn't you do that before?"

"Well, finally you've done it right."

Use Appreciation in Addition to Praise

Appreciation says "I like what you did." It indicates that what a child does, while not extraordinary, is valued. Examples of appreciative statements include:

"I'm glad you changed your shirt—you look neat."

"I appreciate your hanging up your clothes even though you are in a hurry to go out and play."

"I like the way you come in for dinner without being called."

You can also give nonverbal approval messages with a smile, head nod, wink, a gentle squeeze of the hand, a pat on the back, and turning "thumbs up."

Evaluate Your Use of Social Rewards

Although a social reward most often pleases a child, sometimes it can turn him off. If a child has low self-esteem, for example, a social reward may lose credibility because the child can't believe it and feels unworthy. Also, a perfectionistic child may find fault with a social reward because he is not satisfied with his work.

If your child seems to have difficulty accepting your

social reward, be persistent and simply reaffirm the compliment by saying, "Maybe you don't feel that way, but this is the way I feel." Children will also be more likely to accept a social reward if you have a positive relationship with them and if they believe you are trustworthy.

Rewards are the most powerful incentives you have to make your child want to behave. The following summary chart will remind you how to use positive reinforcement effectively.

HOW TO USE REWARDS

Concrete Rewards

1. Use to reinforce desired behavior.
2. Make them contingent upon performing the desired behavior.
3. Be specific.
4. Give them consistently, at first. Then phase them out.
5. Choose appropriate rewards.
6. Use token rewards for immediate feedback, and long-term prizes.
7. Keep a record to help evaluate the reward's effectiveness.

Social Rewards

1. Be specific.
2. Give immediately.
3. Use indirect praise.
4. Use praise in moderation.
5. Don't mix praise and criticism.
6. Use appreciation as well as praise.
7. Evaluate your use of social rewards.

DOING NOTHING

Three-year-old Charlie had a temper. He yelled and kicked his feet when he woke up each morning because he usually didn't like the breakfast his mother prepared; he screamed at playtime when he couldn't find his favorite toy; he threw tantrums each afternoon when he didn't have his mother's undivided attention; he yelled cruel things at his sister whenever she entered the room—and on and on until he fell asleep each night. His parents tried yelling, scolding, and spanking, but the harsher the punishment, the louder and more frequent were Charlie's tantrums.

Finally Charlie's parents had enough; they were tired of being run around in circles by a child who acted like a tyrant. They set up a plan of action that they hoped would change his behavior. To prevent temper tantrums, they created a daily schedule that kept Charlie from being overly bored, tired, or hungry. Then they told Charlie that they would not tolerate his loud outbursts. "When you have a temper tantrum by yelling, kicking, or crying," they told him, "we are not going to look at you or talk to you. The only way you'll be able to get our attention will be to talk nicely and tell us what you want." Then Charlie and his parents practiced the kind of behavior that would be ignored from then on. (Charlie thought it was funny that his parents wanted him to lie on the floor and kick and cry so they could practice ignoring him.) Then they all practiced talking and acting nicely.

For the first two days, the tactic of ignoring them did not stop Charlie's tantrums. In fact, they increased. He would throw himself on the floor and scream so loudly everyone would have to leave the room. He would grab onto his mom's leg and scream as she continued to walk around dragging his body along with her. He would save the loudest outburst for when his dad was on the phone or his mom's friends stopped in for a visit. But his parents never acknowledged the noise. Finally, by the third day, Charlie's tantrums began to subside. He began to talk in a more normal tone of voice when he was upset. Then, just as his parents were congratulating themselves on a job well done, Charlie's grandparents came for a weekend visit. Again, Charlie found an attentive audience for his crying scenes, and his tantrums returned. On Monday morning Charlie lost this audience when his grandparents left and his parents reinstituted their ignoring tactics; by Tuesday afternoon, Charlie again had given up his tantrums. His parents were pleased with the results of their plan and they were determined to have a long talk with Grandma and Grandpa before their next visit.

This story illustrates a do-nothing technique called ignoring.

Ignoring

Most children know that they can wear down their parents' resolve to enforce limits by being persistently difficult until mom or dad says, "Okay. You can have what you want; just stop acting like that." As soon as you or your spouse gives in to your child's negative behavior, you've taught him that his behavior has the power to make you forget about the rules.

The negative behaviors that are most often used by children to get your attention or to get their way are:

clowning	whining
temper tantrums	interrupting
nagging	pleading
using bad language	demanding
clinging	breathholding
crying	

All of these undesirable behaviors can usually be stopped by using a disciplinary strategy called ignoring. Ignoring means deliberately paying no attention to your child in the belief that without an audience your child will have no reason to continue the annoying action. (Of course, you would never ignore any behavior that may be harmful to your child, or others, such as playing with electrical outlets or hitting, or behavior that is destructive, such as spray-painting the cat, or self-rewarding, such as stealing cookies.)

If you choose to ignore a certain behavior, do not look at or talk to your child while he is misbehaving. Give him no attention at all. This means you should avoid

Ignoring

making facial expressions of disapproval, mumbling to yourself, slamming doors, or using angry gestures. You can best ignore your child either by turning your attention to something else or by leaving the room. It will also be easier if you can drown out the sounds of the undesirable behavior by doing things like turning up the TV, putting on stereo headphones, or vacuuming the living room rug. Do whatever you can do to take all your attention away from your child without jeopardizing his safety. (You can't leave town unless you find a babysitter first!)

Like all consequences that are used to enforce limits, you must explain the ignoring technique to your child before you use it. Let him know, for example, that from now on you will not give your attention to anyone who whines. (Be sure to explain exactly what you mean when you use words like "whining," "interrupting," "nagging.") Then explain what kind of behavior will get your attention. Take turns practicing with your child the acceptable behaviors that you want him to use. Pretend you're a child who uses the undesirable behavior that you're trying to eliminate—for example, one who whines to get a glass of juice. (This always brings giggles from kids, who see themselves in their parent's imitation.) Then play a child who knows how to ask for juice nicely, saying, "Mom, may I have a glass of juice now?" Next, ask your child to repeat your performance back to you by asking, "What's the wrong way to ask for something?" Then ask, "What's the right way?" This little game will help your child remember what kind of good behavior will get him the attention he wants. Remember: ALWAYS praise your child when he remembers to use the kind of behavior you're trying to promote.

Because ignoring is a simple procedure, many parents assume that it will be easy to carry out. Unfortunately, it is not. You have to ignore the misbehavior each and every time it occurs. Just paying less attention is not effective and may actually reinforce the misdeed since behavior that is occasionally reinforced is very difficult to extinguish. (That's why people continue to pour money into slot machines even while they're not winning. They know that if they are persistent enough, there's a chance they may win again, as they did two days ago.) The ignoring technique is also easily sabotaged by other people. If grandparents, teachers, siblings, or anyone else can't ignore the behavior you're trying to eliminate, the behavior will not disappear. As long as your child is getting attention from some people, he has no reason to give it up.

To do nothing about your child's misbehaving takes patience and willpower because it's hard to ignore something consistently when it annoys you. Even a fly buzzing at the screen can be ignored only so long before most people will get up and get a fly-swatter. You will need a full reserve of patience, especially when you first begin to use the ignoring technique, because typically, the ignored behavior will get worse before it gets better. If your child is accustomed to getting his way after a five-minute temper tantrum, what do you expect will happen on the first day you decide to ignore it and your child gets no response after five minutes? Most children will assume it means they need to yell louder and longer, and longer, and then longer still. It may take several days before a child will come to realize that the only thing a tantrum will give him is a headache and sore throat.

Most parents who are not prepared for this increase in the negative behavior quickly give up on their efforts to ignore. At a parent-training meeting, one mom flopped back in her seat, and with a wave of her hand completely dismissed the whole idea when another parent asked about the effectiveness of ignoring. "Forget it!" she laughed. "I tried ignoring my son every time he said, 'I hate you.' The only thing that happened was that he started yelling it louder and more often. Ignoring just made things worse."

Ignoring an undesirable behavior will stop it, but it takes time and perseverance. Your efforts will be most effective if you follow these guidelines:

- Set a limit that clearly explains to your child what behavior you will be ignoring.
- Ignore the behavior consistently.
- Make sure everyone in your family (as well as teachers and baby-sitters) agrees to ignore the behavior.

- Expect the undesirable behavior to increase at first.
- Be patient. It may take several weeks before your child really believes that you won't give your attention to his negative behavior. But if you're persistent, he'll get the message eventually.
- Always praise your child when he uses the alternate acceptable behavior.

Learning the Hard Way

Sometimes you can set limits that contain the kind of consequences that you don't have to enforce. These are natural consequences that will teach acceptable behavior when your child realizes that he doesn't like the results of his own actions. This tactic works best with children over three years old because they are better able to understand the cause and effect relationship of their actions.

Situations that might appropriately be handled without enforced consequences include:

"Share your toys with your friend, or she may not want to play with you anymore."

"Put your dirty clothes in the hamper, or you will soon have no clean clothes to wear."

"Eat your lunch now, or you will get very hungry later in the day, and I'm not giving you anything else to eat until suppertime."

Don't be sarcastic when you plan to let your child learn a lesson from natural consequences. Don't say (as maybe your parents did) "Go ahead; break your head and learn the hard way" or "Don't cry to me if you kill yourself falling out of that tree." As with all limits, state in a matter-of-fact tone that if your child breaks the rule, he will have to live with the results. (Like ignoring, this "do nothing" kind of consequence should never be used if the consequences can be harmful to your child, such as swimming toward deep water, or to others, such as throwing rocks, or will be destructive, such as hammering nails into the furniture.)

The most difficult part about letting children learn the hard way is actually letting them do it. After years of looking out for their well-being and protecting them from their own mistakes, it's difficult for most parents to really let children do things like lose friends, run out of clean clothes, or go hungry until suppertime. If you decide to set a rule that will supply its own consequence when it's broken remember: Don't say it unless you're fully prepared to do it. Then, if and when your child has to face the consequence of his actions, your job is done. When he complains to you (and he will) about the situation (the dirty clothes, lost toys, hunger pangs), simply remind him that it was his choice. Don't tag on a scolding; don't nag, threaten, shame, or otherwise rub in the "I told you so" aspect of this discipline tactic. The point is to let your child learn the lesson for himself.

Arlene told her five-year-old son Danny the same thing every day: "Don't leave your toys in the driveway, because they will get run over by a car." But every day Danny forgot the rule and Arlene and her husband had to pick up the scattered toys that blocked the entrance to the garage. Yelling, scolding, and taking away privileges didn't improve Danny's memory. Each night when Danny came in for supper, toys were still in the driveway. Arlene and her husband decided it was time that Danny paid the price for leaving his things where they could be ruined. "We're not going to take your toys out of the driveway anymore," they told him. "If you leave your toys there when you come in for supper, they may get run over by the car, and we will not buy you new ones."

The very next day, Arlene backed her car out of the garage and ran right over Danny's toy truck. Danny cried, and of course blamed his mother for squashing his toy. Arlene remained calm and reminded Danny about the rule and consequence they had talked about the day before. There was no need to holler at him for forgetting or to impose a punishment. Danny had learned a lesson the hard way. From that day on, Danny still needed to be reminded about the rule, but a simple "Remember what happened to your truck" usually did the trick.

STATING A WARNING

If you make a rule, and despite your efforts to help your child abide by it, he breaks the rule, it's time to give him a warning. A warning consists of briefly informing or reminding your child of the consequences he will experience if he continues to misbehave. Sometimes this warning alone will help him behave and spare you the need to impose a penalty.

When you give a warning, don't do it by using vague threats ("You'll be sorry if you keep that up"), doomsday statements ("You'll have your head handed to you if you don't stop"), or idle warnings that you do not intend to enforce. Instead, give a clear, realistic warning that consists of two parts: a statement of misbehavior and the consequence that will certainly be used if the child continues to misbehave. Clear, realistic warnings sound like this:

"This is a warning. If you use that word again, you'll have to go to your room for five minutes."

"I've asked you to stop teasing your sister. If you do it once more, you will not be allowed to watch TV for the rest of the day."

"I'm not going to tell you this again. Either stop complaining or we're going to leave the restaurant. It's your choice."

"You have five seconds to stop crying. If you don't stop by then you'll have to sit on the corner dining room chair until you can stop. One, two, three, four, five."

When you give a warning, don't scream, yell, plead, or threaten your child. Just state the consequences in an unemotional but firm manner. Be sure your tone of voice is firm and carries a negative inflection. Your voice quality—like your message—should be both assertive and disapproving. Otherwise, your child will be confused because your words state the limit, while the wishy-washy tone of your voice says you don't really mean it.

Parents issue warnings in a number of ways; only one of them works. For example, Diane and Tina took their boys to the park one afternoon. Diane's five-year-old son, Tommy, rushed up to the swings and pushed a little girl to the ground. Diane called over to him, and said as she turned the page of her magazine, "Tommy, don't push other children. If you do that again, you're gonna get it." Tommy ran over to the slide and pushed another little boy out of the way and then scurried up the ladder. "I'm warning you," yelled Diane, as she finished her soda, "you do that again and we're going home." Tommy ignored his mother and continued to push and shove his way around the park. "That's it," said Diane again. "You don't get any ice cream when we get home."

When Tina saw Donny, her four-year-old, also push a child to the ground, she stood up, stopped her son in his tracks, looked right into his eyes, and calmly informed him, "If you push another child, we're going home." A few minutes later, Tina saw Donny push another child off the seesaw. Tina immediately said good-bye to Diane, walked over to Donny, reminded him of the warning, and took him home. Following through on the warning was inconvenient for Tina, because she had planned to spend the entire afternoon at the park. But the next time Donny's at the park, he'll know he can't push other children without paying a swift consequence; that should make it easier for Tina to spend a peaceful afternoon. Tommy, on the other hand, will surely still be hurting other children while Diane yells threats at him from across the park. Threats are warnings about dire consequences that you never or rarely carry out. They are designed to intimidate, but children quickly learn to disregard them. A warning on the other hand, is a realistic statement of a consequence that will surely and quickly follow if a misbehavior reoccurs.

To make warnings an effective way to stop misbehaviors in the future, the consequence of an ignored warning should be consistently and immediately administered. Don't repeat a warning ten times before you mean business. Say it only once—and then it's time for action. If the problem behavior is a frequent occurrence that your child knows is not allowed, skip the warning and immediately impose a penalty.

When the warning or penalty is over it's over. Don't drag out the incident with ongoing nagging, reminders, or scoldings. See page 112, "Don't Hold a Grudge," for more about how to end a disciplinary action.

IMPOSING A PENALTY

Penalties are negative consequences. They are the unpleasant things that will happen to your child if he breaks a rule. The use of penalties is the most common form of discipline in most households, yet it is also probably the most controversial topic in child-rearing.

What's a good penalty? How often should it be used? How much is enough? How much is too little? Will my child grow up hating me if I punish him? This kind of question is difficult to answer with absolute certainty because so much depends on the kind of relationship that has developed between the parent and child, on the child's personality, and on the parents' ability to stay in control of their emotions. If you have followed the guidelines in Step One and have established a positive family relationship, your child has learned to care about what you think of his behavior, and you are not prone to violent outburst, then most of your household rules can be effectively enforced by imposing penalties—but only as a last resort.

If you have followed the procedures explained in Steps One and Two, you have already reduced the number of daily discipline problems by improving your relationship with your child, by using preventive techniques, by practicing the alternate strategies explained on page 113, and by setting limits on only a few persistent problem behaviors. As you begin Step Three, first try enforcing those limits by using positive consequences or no-consequence tactics. If these fail to enforce the limits you've set, then it's time to impose penalties.

The following guidelines will give you information about how to use penalties in ways that are effective in changing negative behaviors, yet won't weaken the positive relationship you're building with your child, nor harm his psychological or physical development. These guidelines are followed by a full discussion of five different kinds of penalties in Chapter Seven. You have probably already used some form of each of them. That chapter will teach you ways to maximize the effectiveness.

GENERAL GUIDELINES FOR IMPOSING PENALTIES

Consider Your Child's Developmental Stage

Different kinds of penalties are appropriate at different stages of a child's development. Two-year-olds, for example, are best disciplined with distraction, physical removal, and verbal restrictions, while preschoolers respond better to time-out periods and reprimands.

The appropriate age for each penalty explained in this chapter is included in the discussion. Keep these suggested age limits in mind and be sure to read Appendix A, "Child Development." It will help you understand why some penalties are more appropriate for one particular age than for another.

Be Consistent

Perhaps the most common fault of parents who have problems disciplining children is lack of consistency in enforcement. As explained earlier, consistency is an important factor in setting and enforcing limits, because it makes a child's world more predictable and secure. It is also important because research has found that inconsist-

ent enforcement sometimes actually increases the undesired behavior. If your goal in imposing penalties is to
stop your child's negative behaviors, then make sure you
give the promised penalty every time he breaks the rule.

As in setting limits, you should make sure that all the
people to whom you have given permission to discipline
your child apply the same penalty for the same misbehavior. And as emphasized in the beginning of this chapter,
your child must expect that you will impose a penalty
every time it is warranted. If you punish your child when
he breaks a rule on Monday and then ignore the same
misbehavior on Tuesday, your child has a right to argue
and force you to justify your actions. Arguing over the
rules and their enforcement is a poor approach to
discipline.

The more confident you are in your authority and the
more vigilant you are in applying penalties each time a
particular behavior occurs, the more your child will accept the penalties without protest. Consistency means
rules can be bent only in extraordinary occasions or
emergencies. The sooner children learn that you mean
what you say, that penalties are a certainty for specific
offenses, the better you'll be able to teach your child to
behave.

Disapprove of the Behavior, Not the Child

The message you want to give through punishment is
that, while you disapprove of certain actions, you still
strongly approve of your child himself. Avoid expressing
general disapproval of the whole child by saying things
like "I don't like you for that," or "You're a bad boy."
Keep your reaction limited to specific behaviors, such as
"I don't like your loud screaming in the house."

Through penalties, you want your child to understand
that he made a mistake in judgment for which he must
accept responsibility. He should not feel that he is a bad
or evil person who has terrible faults.

Be Sure the Punishment Is Unpleasant

A punishment must be viewed by your child as an unpleasant experience. So don't, for example, send your child to his room if he thinks it's a fun place to play, or tell him he can't have dessert when he doesn't like cheesecake anyway. For punishment to be effective, your child must find it unpleasant or unsatisfying.

What is unpleasant to one child, however, may be positively reinforcing to another. Studies have shown, for example, that scolding some children can actually increase misbehavior because it is the only form of adult attention they receive. If your child continually misbehaves when you are especially busy or when you are distracted with someone or something else, he may be trying to make you turn your attention toward him, even if your attention comes in the form of punishment. In this case, a child is turning punishment to his advantage. Children often stop these pleas for negative attention when they are assured of an undistracted quality-time period each day.

Remember, though, unless your child finds the penalty unpleasant, it won't be effective. Therefore, you can't really know what is the most effective penalty until you come to really know your child. Take a look back at the quiz on page 19 called "How Well Do You Know Your Child?" The answers will help you determine an appropriate penalty. To determine if a penalty is effective for a misdeed, observe the frequency of the misbehavior to see if it decreases following the consistent application of the penalty. Don't be misled by a child's comments about a particular penalty (e.g., "I don't care if you send me to my room!"); rather focus on whether the misbehavior declines.

Be Reasonable

The punishment you give needs to fit the crime. When you set a limit and state the negative consequence of going beyond it, try to make the penalty logically related to the undesired behavior. For example, if a child mistreats a toy or other possession, that object should be taken from the child for a reasonable period of time.

Also, to ensure that your penalty is reasonable, you should calmly, deliberately, and objectively gather all the relevant facts before you punish your child. If you can adopt a casual approach and try to determine why your child misbehaved, you will be in a better position not only to set a just penalty, but to eliminate the basic cause of the difficulty by understanding the child's motives. Being reasonable doesn't mean, however, that you let your child talk you out of imposing a penalty if it's warranted. Read over "Stand Firm" on page 132. It will arm you against the kind of defenses your child will use to sway your determination to enforce limits.

Be Explicit

In order to avoid any possible misunderstanding by your child about why he is being punished, you should do three things:

1. Name the misbehavior.
2. State the rule that was broken.
3. Describe the penalty that you will impose.

An explicit statement sounds like this: "You decided to go out of the yard today, which is against the rules. Now you'll have to come inside."

By clearly and explicitly linking your child's misbehavior with the penalty, you weaken any of his efforts to blame you for the punishment he has earned. Be sure to emphasize to your child that he had a choice in the situation, and he chose the action that earns a penalty. Your goal should be to promote self-criticism and confession in your child and to prevent him from avoiding responsibility with such tactics as denial ("I didn't do anything wrong"), rationalization ("Everybody is doing it"), or projection ("He started it").

Give Penalties Immediately

Studies have shown that punishment is generally most effective in fostering learning when it immediately follows the misdeed. If more than a few seconds elapse, a young child will have difficulty relating the punishment to the misdeed. Punishment is more effective when it is applied as the child is in the act, for example, of reaching into the cookie jar, rather than after he has eaten them. Delay can cause your child to forget what he did to deserve the penalty.

Be Calm and Matter-of-Fact

Explain a punishment to your child in a calm and matter-of-fact manner, much like a judge reading a decision, or a referee announcing a fifteen-yard penalty in football. Research has shown that the more emotional you are in punishing, the more severe and unreasonable is the punishment you impose. It's also true that when you punish out of hostility, your child will sense this and see the penalty as vengeance rather than justice. So avoid name-calling, yelling, insults, sarcasm, and other judgmental, critical techniques. When you stay in control of yourself, your child will get over his anger much more quickly and will learn you are every bit as serious when speaking firmly as when screaming.

Also, keep in mind that children often pay more attention to the nonverbal communications of the punishing adult than to the verbal ones. So, if you discipline with an enraged look, a vocal tone five times higher than usual, and with trembling hands, your children will feel unloved and disliked, no matter what you say verbally. See page 111 for specific instructions on the use of body language.

It is a goal of the Three-Step Discipline Program always to administer discipline in a firm and confident way. There will probably still be times, however, when you're tempted to punish in the heat of anger. When this happens, take a time-out, get a baby-sitter, go for a walk.

Remind yourself that you can't teach your child self-discipline when you're out of control yourself.

Impose Penalties in Private

No one likes to be criticized in public. When it happens, we react with open or hidden resentment. So a cardinal rule in discipline is that almost without exception, warnings and penalties should be administered as privately as possible.

This doesn't mean that you put off the penalty by saying "You just wait until we get home." Whenever possible, penalties must be given immediately after the rule is broken. But you should make an effort to take your child aside (into another room, out to the car, off to the side) before you impose the promised penalty.

Use Body Language to Your Advantage

Chapter Five described how to use nonverbal cues to assure that your child hears and understands the limits that you set. These same strategies should also be used when imposing penalties.

When your child breaks a rule, don't yell across the yard without looking up from your gardening, "Billy, you know you're not allowed to throw toys. Now go inside until you can behave." You will find that your child will be more responsive to you and to the limits you set if, when a rule is broken, you take the time to go over to your child so you are within three feet of him, squat down to your child's level, look into his eyes and ask him to look back at you, and speak to him in a calm but firm, strong voice.

Allow for the Expression of Feeling

"I hate doing homework."

"All I ever do is clean my room."

These are not "I won't" statements. They are statements of a child's emotional reactions to the rule. Children have a right not to like something. Usually a child will comply with the requirement or take his punishment once he has expressed his displeasure. So allow your children to express their feelings (as long as they don't offend others) and help them to be in touch with these feelings by recognizing them yourself with statements like "It sounds like you really wanted to go to the movies tonight and you feel angry that it's against the rule on school nights."

Don't Hold a Grudge

Young children have a tendency to feel rejected and unloved when punished by their parents. By being friendly and warm to your child after disciplining him you demonstrate that it was the misdeed you disapproved of, not your child. Introduce a positive note as soon as possible by praising your child for taking the penalty well; then redirect your child's attention to an alternate acceptable behavior.

The period after your child has completed a penalty is often a good time to have a heart-to-heart talk about the problem. By being friendly and supportive after imposing a penalty, you can break the negative emotional climate caused by the punishment. Show your child by a hug, praise, or other means that you are eager to relate in enjoyable ways again, and that the incident is closed.

This is not always easy to do. Sandy felt she would be perfectly justified in letting her three-year-old daughter, Christine, sit in her room for the rest of her life. Christine knew that crayons were for drawing on paper only; she had already been punished for drawing on the kitchen floor and on her bedroom door. But this time was more than her mom could stand. When Sandy was in the bathroom, Christine drew all over the beige bricks of the fireplace with purple and red crayons. Sandy immediately administered an appropriate penalty and Christine was very contrite and apologetic, but every time Sandy looked at the fireplace, she was tempted to start scolding all over again. It was difficult for her to let the incident end, but Sandy knew that repeated scoldings and incessant nagging would blur the point she wanted to make, so she took a deep breath and sat down to calmly talk to Christine.

Sandy explained that she was, with good reason, very angry; she talked about the importance of having respect for other people's property. She asked Christine to tell her how she felt about what she had done and about what she planned to do with her crayons in the future. With a reminder that her actions were unacceptable, Sandy gave her daughter a hug and promised herself to drop the subject. Sandy did not feel guilty about punishing Christine for the misdeed, nor did she try to make it up to Christine by giving her a special treat.

Later, Sandy told her husband, "If I hadn't made myself have that talk with Christine, I'd probably be angry for at least another week." By that time Christine would have forgotten what she did wrong and would have transferred the anger to herself and her worth as a daughter. Don't hold a grudge; when the punishment is over, leave the misbehavior in the past.

Point out Acceptable Alternatives

Punishment is designed to teach a child what not to do. A child will be more likely to change his inappropriate behavior, however, when he not only knows what he should not do, but also what he should do. When punishing your child, take the time to explain what you consider to be acceptable behavior in that particular situation: "Blocks are for building things, not for throwing around." Good discipline is a positive force that directs a child toward what he is allowed to do, rather than what he is forbidden to do.

Evaluate the Effectiveness of Your Penalties

Children's reactions to punishment are a very individual thing. Some kids have severe emotional reactions to certain forms of punishment. A very insecure, fearful child, for example, may become quite upset if isolated for a period of time in his room while a more confident child may enjoy the chance to play alone.

Your goal in using a penalty is to stop a negative behavior and replace it with an acceptable one. Watch how your child reacts to the penalty you choose. If it is not teaching him how to behave, take another look at how you are imposing it. If you find that you have used it immediately and consistently, then it is not appropriate for your child. Choose another way to help him behave.

You should also consider your child's feelings about the punishment, since they are as important as the punishment itself. If a child is already feeling remorseful about a mistake, a strong scolding by you may lead to discouragement and depression. In this case, the child needs encouragement rather than criticism. For example, seven-year-old Heather was doing very well in school. She enjoyed learning new things; she always did her homework, and her teacher always wrote on the top of her papers, "Good work." One night, however, Heather wanted to watch a special TV show rather than study for her spelling test, so she told her parents that she didn't have any homework. The following afternoon, Heather came home crying because she had failed her spelling test. Through a gush of tears, she sobbed out the whole story to her mother. She admitted lying about homework so she could watch TV. At first, Heather's mom thought Heather should be punished for lying and for failing her test. But when she considered how upset Heather already was and that she had certainly paid a price for her lie, Heather's mom knew the punishment had already been imposed and that the lesson was well learned.

Chapter 7
Five Kinds of Penalties

There are a variety of penalties that parents can use to punish children. The five types of penalties that follow are those that have been found to be the most acceptable to parents and children, and the most effective in stopping undesirable behaviors.

The discussion of these penalties is followed by a look at the use of spanking. Although spanking is not a recommended penalty, it warrants attention because it is so commonly used.

PENALTY 1: RIGHT THE WRONG

To right the wrong means to make your child aware that what he has done is wrong and that he must make an effort to correct it. This kind of penalty can be used in many situations throughout the day. Most parents exercise the technique every time they tell a child to apologize when he hits another child.

This technique can also be used as the stated consequence in the limits you set before your child gets into trouble. For example, you might say, "You cannot slam the door when you go outside because the rest of the family doesn't like the noise. If you do, you'll have to come back in and close it quietly." Or, "You cannot throw that toy around the room because it will break. If it does break, you will use your allowance money to buy a new one." Very often when your child knows in advance that a misdeed will be followed by work or payment to undo the harm, he will make an effort to obey the rule.

Righting wrongs is a penalty that can be used with children three years old and older. It helps them restore a sense of self-worth and also the good will of others. Making amends can also teach children to consider how others are affected by their actions. It helps a child learn that when he hurts someone, or infringes on someone's rights, he should do something to correct it. Righting wrongs, therefore, is an altruistic rather than a punitive form of punishment.

Example

Five-year-old Glenn and his friend Sean were playing baseball in Glenn's backyard. When Glenn's dad, Ray, came home he waved a hello and yelled over his shoulder, "Keep your eye on the ball," Sean was winding up the pitch; Glenn tightened his grip on the bat and then swung with all his might. Two seconds later, Glenn saw his first line drive whirl right through Mrs. Cavanaugh's kitchen window. As the glass shattered, Sean ran home, and Glenn ran inside crying, "I didn't mean it. I didn't mean to do it."

Although his first reaction was to yell, Glenn's dad bit his lip. Ray realized that it was certainly an accident, and since he had never told Glenn not to play ball in the yard, it wouldn't be right to punish him now. This broken window gave Ray the chance to show Glenn the right thing to do in this kind of situation and to set a limit to keep it from happening again.

Ray took Glenn's hand and together they walked over to Mrs. Cavanaugh's. As Glenn hung his head in fear and guilt, Ray explained how the accident happened; he apologized for Glenn and promised to buy new glass and fix the window right after supper.

Right the wrong

During supper, Ray calmly set this new limit on Glenn's baseball playing: "You can play baseball, but only in the park. You can't play in the backyard because you may break more windows. If you play in the yard and another window gets broken, you will go by yourself to apologize to that neighbor; you will use your allowance money to pay for new glass, and instead of going out to play with your friends, you will come with me to fix it."

Now that the limit is set and the consequence is clear, there won't be any need for yelling, threatening, or hitting if Glenn should break another window. Glenn's dad can simply remind him that it's his responsibility to right the wrong.

PENALTY 2: LOSE A PRIVILEGE
OR POSSESSION

This kind of penalty says to your child, "If you do
something bad, you will lose something that you like."
The time-honored discipline tactic of "grounding" is an
example of this penalty. If a child breaks a rule, he loses
his right to go out and play. This penalty may be effectively used with children ages two and a half and over.
Some parents also use this kind of penalty when they
withhold part of their child's allowance if he doesn't do
his assigned chores. Loss of TV or video game time is
another privilege that is often withheld as a consequence
for breaking the rules.

When you set a limit that uses loss of a privilege or
possession as a consequence, make sure the loss will be
unpleasant for your child, yet at the same time will be
realistically enforceable. Taking away the right to watch
TV on a night when there's nothing your child likes to
watch won't effectively control his future behavior. On
the other hand, you don't want to overdo it by making
the loss too extreme or too complex for you to consistently follow through. Taking away dessert for one month,
for example, is too long a period of time for your child to
connect the misdeed to the punishment. Taking away all
your child's toys because he broke one of them will probably only multiply your discipline problems—because now
he has nothing to play with. And if you take away your
child's right to watch TV for two weeks, you'll most
likely give in after only a few days.

Make the consequence of lost privilege or possession
unpleasant, realistic, and quick. Use loss of TV only
when your child's favorite show is on that night. Take
away a snack only when you have something on hand he
really likes. And don't take away all of his toys at once;
pick up only the toys that weren't put away when they
should have been and store them in a "Saturday Box" for
toys that can't be played with again until Saturday.

Example

Julie had penalized her two older children with loss of privileges and possessions many times. "It never worked," she said. "Now, with my youngest one, I've finally found out what I had been doing wrong all those years and why the kids never seemed to mind when I took away their privileges. I didn't talk to them ahead of time and explain what the consequence would be if they broke a rule. After the rule was broken, I would be so angry, I'd yell out some extreme punishment that I thought would really impress on them how wrong they were. I'd take away their favorite snack for a week, their favorite stuffed animal for a month, their favorite toy forever. But they never seemed to really care; the misbehavior would continue—I guess because they knew I'd soon give back the privilege or possession anyway. Now that I've learned how to use this penalty correctly, my littlest one knows I mean business and it really works to keep her in line.

"Right now, for example, Katlyn knows that if she throws a toy, I will take it away from her for the rest of the day. If she jumps on the couch while she's watching TV (that's one of her favorite activities), I will turn off the TV for one hour. This way, I've set limits and reasonable consequences in advance that I know I can and will enforce. Katlyn knows it too."

PENALTY 3: A BRIEF SCOLDING

A discussion of penalties would not be complete without mention of scolding. It's the discipline tactic most often used each day in every American home. From the first time a baby creeps toward an electrical outlet, voicing loud disapproval seems to be an inborn parental reaction. Unfortunately, scoldings often become so commonplace, so drawn out, and so dramatic that they lose their power to control behavior. You need to develop a method of scolding that will satisfy your need to respond to negative behavior verbally, and at the same time help teach your child to behave.

Effective scoldings follow the guidelines for imposing penalties that are explained on pages 106–114. For example: A scolding should be given in a private place and face to face. It should use words that are specific to the misdeed. (Wrong: "Stop clowning around." Right: "You are not allowed to roll your peas off your brother's head."). It should focus on the child's behavior, not the child. Wrong: "You're a bad boy." Right: "Throwing sand at your friend is a bad thing to do."). Review all the guidelines. They will help you begin to reevaluate the way you reprimand your child.

Next, set a limit on how long your scoldings will last. One minute is usually plenty of time to get across your message of disapproval. Anything over that time turns into a lecture, and lectures have the power to make most children become deaf instantly. In one minute, you can easily follow this six-step method of effective scolding:

1. Point out the specific problem behavior that must be changed: "Do not climb on top of the table."
2. Explain the reason for the limit with an "I-message." This kind of message is explained in Tom Gordon's book, *Parent Effectiveness Training*. It is a message that states your feelings about the negative behavior and why you want it stopped: "I feel irritated when you play your drums too loudly because it gives me a headache." I-messages keep your child from feeling victimized or constantly blamed for everything. ("You are too noisy." "You are giving me a headache.") Often children don't realize *why* something bothers their parents, since they see things only from their own perspective. I-messages are especially effective in families where there is a positive family relationship, and the children have learned to care about how their parents feel.
3. If you have already set a limit on this disruptive behavior, continue the scolding by enforcing the consequence that has been agreed upon: "I told you

that if you lied to me one more time you would not be allowed to play with your video games for the rest of the day. Now give me all your game cartridges. I'll give them back to you tomorrow."

If you have not already set a limit on this behavior, continue the scolding by telling your child what the consequence will be if he continues to misbehave. "If you lie to me again, you will not be allowed to play with your video games for the rest of that day."

4. Point out an acceptable alternative: "Instead of throwing sand at your friends, put the sand into this bucket."
5. Make sure your child understands why you're scolding him: "Do you understand what you did wrong? Tell me why you're being scolded."
6. Reestablish affectionate bonds with your child as soon as possible after the scolding. If he responds to your reprimand and changes his behavior, comment on that: "Thank you for handling the cat so gently."

   If he does not respond and you must impose a penalty, find something nice to say about that. "I like the way you cleaned up your own mess."

A scolding that covers these six steps can be given in less than sixty seconds, like this:

1. "Do not splash water out of the bathtub."
2. "I feel angry when I have to clean up the water that gets all over the floor."
3. "If you continue to splash, you will have to stay in the bathroom and clean it up—even if that means missing your favorite TV show."
4. "Here is a water toy that you can play with without splashing."
5. "Do you understand what I want you to do? Tell me."
6. "Thank you for playing so nicely without splashing."

Once you've covered the six steps—stop! Drop it. The scolding is over. Don't even allow your spouse to reprimand again for this misdeed at a later time. An effective scolding is a brief, one-time ordeal that will keep you on the subject, prevent you from lecturing, and make it impossible for you to bring up past wrongs that have nothing to do with the specific problem. ("And another thing, I asked you to clean up your room this morning and you didn't. I'm sick and tired of the way you ignore me. Even your father says you're getting lazy. And . . .")

You never need to yell. This may seem like a contradiction in terms—scolding without yelling?—but the purpose of scolding is to show your disapproval and to teach your child how to change his misbehaviors to acceptable ones. It's not necessary or effective to yell out this kind of message. Use an assertive tone of voice with a stern look on your face that tells your child you mean business. But don't shout, shriek, scream, nag, or use a hostile tone of voice. This will only alienate your child.

The next time you take that deep breath that comes just before you intend to yell at your child, hold it in. Count to ten, and try using the six-step brief scolding described above.

PENALTY 4: TIME-OUT

In sports, a time-out is a brief interruption of the action. In discipline, a time-out is an interruption of your child's disruptive behavior. Time-out is related to the loss-of-privilege penalty, but instead of taking the abused toy away from your child, for example, time-out would require that you take your child away from the toy.

Time-out is a technique that you can use to stop a negative behavior by removing your child from the area of trouble and placing him in an isolated area. This is effective because it immediately stops the misdeed. It is unpleasant for a child because it takes away his freedom to play and interact with his family and friends. And it is safe because it serves as a cooling-off period for both the child and the parent. The child is given time to think about the misbehavior, and it gives the parents a chance to regain control of their emotions so they don't punish in the heat of anger.

Time-out can effectively stop behaviors that are especially aggressive, impulsive, or hard to handle. These include:

hitting	cursing and swearing
temper tantrum	throwing dirt or rocks
toy throwing	biting
disobedience	kicking
destructiveness	teasing
hair pulling	hurting pets
name calling	interrupting
spitting	fights
whining	clowning around

The Time-Out Place

Choose a place in your house where your child will go every time you enforce time-out. It should be a place away from the action, a place that is boring (no TV, books, games, toys) a place where the child won't get any attention from other family members, and a place that your child can get to quickly. A straight-backed chair set apart from the action is often best. Remember that for a penalty to be effective, it must be unpleasant for your child.

If you're visiting in someone else's home when you need to enforce a time-out, try to find a secluded place for your child to go. If, however, there is a chance that your child might break or damage something during the time-out, keep him in sight or send him out into the hallway, onto the porch, or out in the yard. If you are in a public place, use an out-of-the-way bench, corridor, restroom, or even your car to impose the time-out. The time-out rules for public places are the same as at home with the exception that you should not leave your child alone. Although you will still ignore him and withhold your attention, keep him well in sight.

Try not to use the following places for time-out:

- *Bedroom.* There are too many fun things to do in this room, and it is never wise to associate punishment with the place your child sleeps. Going to sleep is difficult enough for some children because of the separation anxieties it invokes. Don't reinforce the idea that there is something bad about the bedroom.
- *Bathroom and kitchen.* There are too many potentially dangerous objects in these rooms. A bored child may begin to search for something to do and come up with razor blades, knives, hot water taps, or stove control knobs.
- *Dark closets or basements.* These places are too scary to be used for time-out. The goal is not to scare your child into obedience; it is to immediately stop an inappropriate behavior and take away something—in this case, freedom—that your child wants.

If your child still suffers separation anxiety when you leave him, it is probably best to use a time-out place in the living room or dining room where he won't feel too isolated.

The Time-Out Method

When your child breaks a rule that he knows has time-out consequences, send him to the time-out place. Don't argue; don't negotiate. In ten words or less remind him of the rule and its consequences. (Time-out will not work if you wait too long, as in: "Your teacher said you talked back to her this morning. Now go to time-out.")

If your child resists, use physical assistance; pick him up or direct his steps to bring him quickly to the time-out place. State the amount of time he must stay there. (See the first tip, which follows.) Remind him that if he is not quiet by the end of time-out, the time of his confinement will be extended until he is calm. Offer him an alternate acceptable behavior that he can use the next time he's in the same situation. Welcome your child back as soon as time-out is over.

Time-out

Time-out Tips

• A general rule of thumb says, keep your child in time-out one minute for every year of age. A two-year-old therefore would stay only two minutes, while an eight-year-old will stay eight.

- Pretend you can't hear any of the mean things your child says about you during his stay in time-out.
- Place a portable kitchen timer near your child to mark the time your child stays in time-out. It will help you be fair and consistent. It cannot be talked into giving in early. It won't forget to signal your child when time is up, (as parents sometimes do). It will keep your child from pestering you by repeatedly asking, "Is time up yet?" It's best to use a portable timer that can be placed where your child can hear it ticking and can hear when time is up. (Keep it out of reach, however, so your child can't set the time forward.)
- It may be necessary to firmly hold your preschooler in the chair if he tries to escape. Don't show him your anger; just do it and keep counting. If your child gets up out of the time-out chair, escort him back and reset the timer back to the beginning every time he does it. He'll soon learn that the only way to get out of time-out is remain there until his penalty time is up.
- Time-out is an effective way to stop undesirable behaviors. It should *not* be used as a motivation to get your child to start a task. ("You didn't clean your room this morning. Do it now, or you'll have to go to the time-out place.")
- Your child needs to know in advance what time-out is and how it works. Explain that time-out will be used every time he misbehaves in a certain way. Tell him where he will go and how long he will stay.
- Don't use time-out too often. If you put your child in time-out for all his negative behaviors, he may spend his entire day there. Choose only one or two negative behaviors that you will punish with time-out, and then consistently use it everytime your child breaks that rule. In the beginning he may very well spend the majority of his day in the time-out place if it's a persistent problem, but by the second day you'll

find you need to use it less, and the third day even less, until eventually, the negative behavior will be under control.

Example

Irene brought two-year-old Jason to a toddler play-gym. Jason loved it. He had lots of room to run, and jump, and slide, and fall. No one cared how loudly he squealed, laughed, or yelled. Irene was delighted to see how much fun Jason was having, when without warning Jason ran up to another young boy and slapped him on the head. Irene ran over, apologized to the boy and his mother, and took Jason aside to a corner of the room. She squatted down to his level, put her hands on his shoulders, looked him in the eye, and in a stern disapproving voice told him, "You are not allowed to hit the other children. If you do," she warned him, "you'll have to stop playing and sit right here in the corner for two minutes. Okay?" she asked. "Okay," mumbled Jason.

Jason ran off to play with the colorful bouncing balls that were rolling around the gym. When a little girl picked up the one that Jason has his eye on, he reached out and hit her on the back. Irene went over to him, apologized to the girl and her mother, and escorted a crying Jason back to the corner. She reminded him of the rule, and told him he must stay in the corner until time-out was over. Jason continued to cry because he wanted to play, but Irene turned away from him and patiently waited out the promised two minutes. When time was up, Irene turned back to Jason, warned him not to hit the other children, and sent him back out to play.

Anxious to make up for lost time, Jason ran out onto the gym floor. He climbed to the top of the slide and promptly swatted another little boy in the face. Irene repeated her apology, and again brought Jason to the corner of the gym for time-out. Knowing his mom was really going to make him sit there, Jason cried even louder this time. Despite the embarrassment of again sitting in the corner with a screaming child, Irene stood firm for the full two minutes. When time was up, Irene took Jason back to the play area. She stayed close by and encouraged him to play nicely with the hoops. "I'm so happy to see you having fun without hitting the other children," she told him. For the rest of the play time, Irene praised Jason every time he came close to another child without hitting him.

When play-gym was over, Irene hugged and kissed Jason and complimented him on playing so nicely. She told him they could come back in two days to play again.

What Irene didn't tell Jason was that she knew it would take several more visits to the time-out corner before he learned that hitting other children was wrong and would cause him to lose play time.

PENALTY 5: PHYSICAL ASSISTANCE

Since you are responsible for your child and his actions, there may be times when you cannot tolerate his open defiance and refusal to cooperate. That's when it may become necessary for you to use physical assistance to show your child that you mean what you say. This kind of penalty should be used only when all other types of discipline have failed however.

Parents sometimes claim, "I've tried everything to control this child; nothing works." Most often this happens because the parents are unsure how to discipline and they aren't consistent in their approach. In these cases following the three-step discipline program will usually solve the dilemma. If, however, you take time to establish a positive family relationship, set reasonable limits in advance of the problem, properly use positive, natural, and negative consequences, and *still* your child screams, "I won't do it! You can't make me!"—then it's time to show him that since you're in charge, you can.

Let's say, for example, that the rule in your house says your four-year-old must come inside at 5:00 P.M. every night. No matter what kind of consequence you use, however, your child steadfastly refuses to come in. Calmly, without hostility, yet with determination, go outside, pick his body up, and bring it in. Now he knows you're in control. If your child has been told he must hang up his own coat, but he still drops it on the floor and refuses to hang it up, take his hands, pull them down to the coat, bend his fingers around the material, walk him and the coat over to the closet, and guide his hands to put the coat in its proper place. If your child knows he has to clean up his toys before bedtime, but then refuses to do it, physically guide him to each toy. Bend him over. Help him pick each one up and deposit it wherever it belongs.

When you use physical assistance, don't yell, or scold, or show your anger; remember, this gives your child attention and sometimes satisfaction. Use only as much assistance as necessary to complete the task. Stay calm and show him that without a doubt, you can make him follow the rules. After a few such episodes, he will do it himself since he now knows you'll make him do it anyway.

A WORD ABOUT PHYSICAL PUNISHMENT

Physical punishment (spanking, hitting, slapping, whipping, beating) is not part of this three-step discipline program. Since the other methods of discipline explained in this program are more effective in teaching a child to behave, there is no reason to include these aggressive approaches. But surveys commonly find that approximately 90 percent of today's parents still use spanking and other means of physical punishment to discipline their children. This is surprising in light of the following:

Physical punishment does NOT
- Encourage children to develop self-control
- Nurture a close parent/child relationship
- Guide children to choose right over wrong instinctively
- Teach children the logical and natural results of misbehaving
- Change negative behavior to acceptable behaviors in the long run

Furthermore, physical punishment MAY
- Make children angry, hostile, fearful
- Teach that violence is a way to handle problems
- Lead to physical and emotional abuse
- Show children that you don't believe in the Golden Rule ("Do unto others as you would have them do unto you.")
- Break down the positive kind of family interaction that is developed in Step One of this program
- Teach that it's okay to vent anger by hurting others

Despite this information, some parents still believe that physical punishment should be used on occasion. Since this is so, these parents should know how to use this kind of penalty in a way that is least likely to harm the child physically or psychologically. The following are guidelines for giving a "quick lick" spanking that will not turn into a beating:

- Spank with an open hand, never with your fist or an object (a belt, spoon, ruler, hairbrush).
- Hit only on the buttocks or hands, not on any other part of the body.
- Never slap your child in the face.
- Give only one quick hit. After that it becomes a beating.
- Don't react in initial anger. Use physical punishment only when you have complete emotional control.
- Never hit more than once a day.
- Never use physical punishment to penalize aggressive behaviors like hitting, biting, kicking, or fighting.
- Never spank an infant, or a child over the age of ten.
- Never allow anyone else to spank your child—not brothers, sisters, grandparents, aunts or uncles, or baby-sitters.
- Never shake your child. It can inflict lasting damage to a young child's brain, and recent research findings have shown that whiplash effects are not uncommon following the shaking of a child. The whiplash can be severe enough to cause damage to the brain and the vertebrae of the neck.

Of course, the best advice is: Don't do it.

Most parents do not want to hit their children and they feel terrible after they do it. Usually these parents use physical punishment only because they can't think of a better way to correct their child at that moment. But after reading this book you can see that since there are so many other discipline strategies you can use, there is no reason to use one that has such negative short- and long-term effects. The next time you're tempted to raise your hand to physically punish your child, STOP! Remind yourself that hitting will not really solve the problem. Then use one of the other consequences or penalties discussed earlier in this book.

Chapter 8
Stand Firm

These four methods of enforcing limits—rewards, doing nothing (ignoring and letting natural consequences take over), issuing warnings, and penalties—are proven and effective techniques that will help you teach your child how to behave. Remember, however, that you must stand firm in your resolve to use them immediately and consistently. If you promise your child a special treat when he eats his whole supper, don't give it to him unless he eats the meal. If you're determined to teach your child a lesson by letting his laundry pile up in his room, don't break down and do it after the first few days. If you warn your child that you will impose a penalty if he breaks a certain rule and then he breaks it, you must use the promised punishment.

You can be sure that your child will not initially love the three-step program of discipline. In fact, he will quickly develop a hefty repertoire of tactics to talk you out of it. The following list will give you just an inkling of what your child will do to make you change your mind, give in, or even give up this discipline program. Be prepared for them. Take them in stride, and then stand firm and impose the promised consequence.

Name-calling

Your child knows how to make you feel guilty by calling you all the things you're trying not to be. He can easily undermine your confidence with quick phrases like:

"I hate you."

"Mean Mommy."

"You're ugly."

"You don't love me."

Temper Tantrums

These may include screaming, kicking, throwing things, spitting, and head banging. In fact, the tantrum may be worse than the negative behavior you were trying to change.

Denial

This is an all-time favorite that kids hope will make their parents doubt themselves: "I didn't do it."

Breathholding

This is a scary one. Most parents will give in when their child's face begins to turn blue and his eyes start to bulge. Don't fall for it. Just sit your child in a soft chair because the absolute worst that can happen is that he'll pass out and start breathing again. If you ignore him while he's holding his breath, he won't do it too many more times. If you give in because of it, he'll do it every time you try to enforce a limit.

Crying

Most children will cry when the rules are enforced. Some children, however, will wail and sob hysterically.

They will lose their breath; they will go on for what seems an eternity. Some children get so hysterical that they even vomit. (If that happens, just clean up the mess and continue to stand firm.) If all that these children get for their efforts is a headache, they'll soon stop. If they get their own way, you've created a sobbing monster.

Whining

That nasally piercing sound that has the innate ability to drive all parents crazy in the first three minutes of use is a hard one to ignore—but do it anyway, or you'll be hearing more of it.

Comparisons

Propaganda is your child's best friend. He will try to convince you that you must be wrong since no one else agrees with you. His two favorite lines will be:

"Johnny's mother lets him do it."

"Daddy always lets me do it" (or "Mommy" depending on who's doing the disciplining at the moment).

Defiance

A strong-willed child will challenge you and your decision to enforce a limit by trying to overpower your position of authority. He will stand firm with such simple but intimidating statements as, "I won't do it. You can't make me!" He says this in the hope that you will be the one to back down. Don't. If necessary use physical assistance, as described on page 128.

Threats

For every threat you may have used in the past to make your child obey you, he has created an additional three to make you change your mind. Do not be surprised or swayed when you hear:

"I'm never going to love you anymore."

"I'm going to run away and you'll be sorry."

"I'm telling Mommy on you."

The Silent Treatment

Children know the power of silence. When they pout, sulk, or ignore you, you'll feel as if you've crushed their soul and destroyed their joyful spirit. Don't be a pawn; they're just showing you another side of their dramatic spirit.

Promises

The goal of enforcing limits is to foster good behavior in the future. So if your child promises you "I'll be good" and begs for "One more chance," it's hard to say no. Do it anyway. If you had to bet which method would guarantee obedience in the future, enforcing the limit or giving in, which one would you put your money on?

Excuses

Sometimes your child may have a valid reason for not doing what you ask him to do. It's your job to learn the difference between a valid reason and a poor excuse. Can you tell which is which?

"I didn't walk the dog because I didn't have time."

"I didn't walk the dog because you put the leash up on the top of the closet, and I couldn't reach it."

"I didn't clean my room because I forgot you asked me to."

"I didn't clean my room because I had a terrible headache and when I lay down on the bed, I fell asleep."

"I didn't do my homework because the dog ate my pen."

"I didn't do my homework because that was the night we had the storm and lost electrical power."

(If you're not sure, in all three pairs the top statements are excuses and the bottom ones are reasons.)

There is probably only one thing for certain when you attempt to enforce limits, and that is that your children will try to make you change your mind. The fact that a rule makes them unhappy or frustrated does not make you a "bad" parent. If you're sure your rules and their consequences are fair, then stand firm. Temporary unpopularity with your children is the price you sometimes have to pay for being a good parent.

PART II

Discipline in Action

Chapter 9
Parents with Problems

Over the years, parents have invented ingenious ways to discipline their children. Some are very effective; some are questionable; some are plain useless; and some are even dangerous. Most of them, however, have the same immediate goal: to stop the noise and misbehavior and replace it with obedience—*now*. Most discipline techniques will do this, but good discipline techniques will do this *and* help your child develop self-control and self-direction *and* enable him to grow into a secure adult who can relate well to those around him. All parents want this for their children, but because discipline techniques are often selected at random and used in haphazard ways, many children are raised with disciplinary strategies that inhibit the very goals their parents aim for.

The most obvious example of a parent with problems is one whose disciplinary methods result in child abuse. Some studies indicate that child abuse has become an epidemic that is caused by a total breakdown in the disciplinary process. Child abusers are often found to be ineffective disciplinarians whose children are totally out of control. Many of these parents physically hurt their children in the name of discipline by beating, hitting, burning, and sometimes even killing them. Others abuse their children verbally by ridiculing, insulting, belittling, and ultimately killing the child's spirit. These parents need to know that there are other methods of discipline they can use when they feel at wit's end and are tempted to use physical or verbal beatings to make their children behave.

There are many more parents who have problems disciplining their children, but their need for help is not so obvious. The negative impact of being too permissive or too harsh, for example, may not be noticeable for many years. Studies have found that parents who overindulge their children and those who don't set down any rules in the belief that their children should learn from their own mistakes often produce adults who are spoiled, selfish, inconsiderate, demanding, and act out in an antisocial and aggressive manner. On the other hand, children who are raised by overly harsh, strict, and dictatorial parents show characteristics of rebelliousness and socially deviant behavior. These children often have a poor sense of initiative and responsibility and low self-esteem, and they usually develop a fear and hatred of the punishing person which may extend to anyone in a position of authority.

This kind of long-term effect makes it clear that the kind of disciplinary approach you choose should not be left to chance. A number of commonly used yet totally ineffectual leadership strategies are presented in the following character descriptions. Read through them all and see if any of them describe you and the way you presently respond to your children. Although all parents use some of these methods at one time or another, if any of these descriptions closely match your day-to-day approach to discipline problems, pay particular attention to the suggested "Remedy" when you implement the three-step program of discipline in your home. Page reference numbers are given to direct you to the original discussion of each suggested discipline tactic.

Olivia Ostrich

PROBLEMS IN PARENTING STYLES

Olivia Ostrich

Olivia pretends she can't see or hear her children when they're misbehaving. She acts as if she believes: "If you don't pay any attention to a discipline problem, it will go away." You probably saw Olivia at your last large family gathering. She sat in the living room talking, laughing, and nibbling at the hors d'oeuvres while her kids wreaked havoc throughout your house. They were disruptive, rude, and destructive, but Olivia never noticed.

Remedy: Olivia won't be able to discipline her children until she has a complete change of attitude. She must see discipline as her parental responsibility and something that her children cannot do without if she expects them to grow into emotionally healthy people. Then Olivia can trade in her avoidance style for the active approach in the three-step program.

Nick the Nagger

Nick is a verbal beggar. He wants his kids to do their chores and to be responsible for themselves, so he spends each day reminding them what they should do. But when each day ends, the chores are still left undone. A typical Saturday at Nick's house goes something like this:

Nick: "Jane, I want you to help your mom put away the laundry."

Jane: "Okay, right after this TV show."

Nick: "Tom, get the clay out of your rug."

Tom: "In a little while; I'm doing something."

Nick: "Jane, what about the laundry?"

Jane: "In a minute, this show is almost over."

Nick: "Tom, that clay is going to ruin the rug if it dries there."

Tom: "Don't worry, I'll get to it later."

Nick: "Jane, remember what I told you. Tom, don't forget."

Nick: "Jane, you'd better get in here. Tom, I'm warning you."

Nick: "Jane, let's go. Tom, you'd better listen to me. "You kids never help out around here."

Remedy: Nick has to take control by following through on his directives. If Jane doesn't help her mother put away the laundry the first time he asks her to, it's time for a warning: "Jane, if you don't help your mother by the time I count to three, you will not be allowed to watch any TV for the rest of the day. One, two, three." (See page 80). Then Nick has to follow through and watch that she does the job, and if she doesn't, he has to make sure she doesn't watch any TV until the next day. The same procedure will convince Tom to clean up the clay. Nick will find his kids will help around the house if he consistently gives a directive and then follows through and rewards them when the job is done, or penalizes them when it isn't.

Tina Tongue-lasher

Tina disciplines with verbal attacks. Nothing is out of bounds; she feels justified in using a variety of approaches like:

- *sarcasm:* "Where were you born, in a barn?"
- *ridicule:* "If you're so smart, why don't you get good grades in school?"
- *name-calling:* "You clumsy idiot."
- *belittling remarks:* "You can't do anything right."
- *shame:* "Shame on you. I told you not to take that cookie and you did anyway."

Tina would never physically abuse her children, but she doesn't realize that her persistent tongue-lashings are another form of child abuse. In fact, in most states she could be legally prosecuted for inflicting emotional injury on her children.

The Committee for the Prevention of Child Abuse has waged a media campaign to raise public awareness about the dangers of verbal abuse. These ads (like the one that follows) strive to get the word out that verbal abuse can undermine a child's personality and lead to long-term problems.

Remedy: Tina has to redirect her anger at her children's negative behaviors rather than at the children themselves. (See page 107.) She also has to learn to bite her tongue and count to ten before she says anything derogatory to her children. (If parents like Tina can't stop their verbal attacks, they should seek professional help.)

Children believe what their parents tell them.

Words hit as hard as a fist.
Next time, stop and listen to what you're saying.
You might not believe your ears.

Take time out. Don't take it out on your kid.
Write: National Committee for Prevention of Child Abuse. Box 2866E. Chicago. IL 60690

Ed the Exaggerator

Ed is in the habit of projecting his children's misdeeds onto some kind of global scorecard. He tackles all discipline problems with nonsensical exaggerations like:

"You never listen to me."

"You always lie."

"You never do what you say you will."

Ed's kids are starting to believe what he says, and they act accordingly.

Remedy: Ed has to learn to be specific in his complaints and deal with the problem he faces at the moment—not what happened yesterday, or what will probably happen tomorrow. (See page 70.)

Sue the Screamer

Sue pierces all discipline problems with loud shrieks. All misdeeds, whether minor or severe, get the same response. At first, her children were frightened by her screaming tirades. Now they don't seem to mind at all; in fact, they don't even hear her anymore. (Only the neighbors are bothered by her loud style of parenting.) Sue has confided to a friend, "My kids are so bad that they don't care how often, how loud, or for how long I yell at them. They just keep misbehaving." Sue's kids aren't so bad; Sue's style of discipline is.

Remedy: Sue has to stop yelling. She also has to learn how to ignore some misbehaving so that when she does correct her children they'll know it's for something that really matters. (See page 97.) Little by little, Sue must try to get through her days without *any* loud reprimands. She should practice staying in control and giving *brief* scoldings for breaking house rules (as explained on pages 119–122). It won't be long before Sue's children are listening to her again—and *then* she can begin to teach them how to behave.

Chuck the Chaser

When Chuck sees his kids misbehaving, he doesn't just sit there. He gets right up and runs after them. He chases them through the living room, across the kitchen, and up the stairs. He lets them know that if he catches them, they're in big trouble. Sometimes he even picks up a wooden spoon on his jaunt through the kitchen and waves it in the air as a harbinger of the painful reprisal yet to come.

When his kids see him coming they squeal with delight, and the chase is on. They slide under tables, slam doors behind them, and hide behind their mother. It's the most fun they'll have all day. The chase usually ends when they beat their dad to their bedroom and lock him out in the hall. Then Chuck yells through the door, "You kids better not come out of there or you're gonna get it!" Then he retreats back to the living room.

Chuck could probably catch his kids if he really wanted to, but he doesn't because he figures that this way they know he won't just sit back when they misbehave, and he puts an immediate stop to the misdeed, and they end up out of sight in their room. Chuck's happy with that arrangement.

Remedy: Although Chuck is happy with his chasing strategy, it is not helping his kids learn how to behave. It may stop misbehavior for the time period of the chase, but it does nothing to help his children learn what they should do.

Chuck has created a game that his kids love to play. It will take some time and patience to make them realize that the rules to the discipline game have changed. But Chuck can't teach them the new rules the very next time they misbehave, because as he approaches to talk to them they'll automatically run away. He needs to sit them down in advance of trouble and make it clear that the chasing game is over. He must then set a limit something like this: "When I want to talk to you, you must stay still and listen." And then he should set up a consequence something like this: "If you do that, you will make me very proud of you. If you run away from me, I will be very disappointed, but I will not chase you. You will each lose one hour of outdoor playtime." (See page 118.)

Out of habit, and with a need to test the new rule, Chuck's kids will probably run away the next time he approaches to punish them. When that happens, Chuck can sit back and relax. Without yelling, scolding, or hitting he can enforce his limit by keeping them inside when they come running back to him asking to go out and play. His kids will soon stop running away, because running away will result in a negative consequence and because it's no fun to run away if no one chases after you.

Connie Comparer

Connie would like her four-year-old to behave as nicely as her six-year-old. Her discipline technique focuses on pointing out to the younger one what the older one does and does not do in the same situation.

In the morning, she says, "Look, your brother is already dressed and you're still sitting there in your pajamas. Why can't you be more like him?"

In the afternoon, she says, "I never had to worry about your brother leaving his belongings at nursery school. With you it's an every-day problem."

In the evening, she says, "Your brother has eaten all his vegetables already. You can not leave the table until you do the same."

At bedtime she says, "Why are your toys the only ones I see cluttering up this bedroom? I don't see any of your brother's. Why is it that he can put things away, but you can't?"

Connie has turned every problem of the day into a case for sibling rivalry.

Remedy: Although older children do often serve as models for the younger ones to imitate (both good and bad behaviors) Connie is using unfavorable comparisons in an attempt to control behavior through ridicule, shame, and belittling. She must learn to stop seeing her younger child as a miniature version of the older one. They are each unique human beings who need to be seen as individuals with personal characteristics, needs, and behavior patterns separate from each other. (See page 27.)

Connie should first make an effort to look for positive things that make the younger one different than his brother (a winning smile, a love of animals, an artistic talent). This will help individualize her attention toward him. Then she must learn to address each discipline problem as a unique situation, totally separate from her other child. She must understand that what the older child does or does not do has nothing to do with the problem at hand. Connie may be more willing to change her motivational approach when she realizes that it is causing the younger one to feel inferior and is creating a barrier of resentment and hostility between the two of them.

Walter the Withholder

Walter punishes his children by withholding a part of himself from them. For lying to him, he may give them the silent treatment for days. For talking back to him, he may suddenly become too busy to give them the attention they want (Child: "Can I have some juice?" Walter: "I'm busy. You're so smart; get it yourself.") Or, when really angry, Walter will withhold his love and wait for his children to beg for it back with promises to be good. (Walter: "I don't love you anymore. You don't listen to me." Child: "I'm sorry, Daddy. Please love me. I'll be good. I promise.")

Remedy: Although Walter can control negative behaviors by withholding a privilege or a possession, he can't do it by withholding a part of himself. He is hurting his relationship with his children and doing little to change their behavior because he is attacking the children, not their misdeeds. (See page 107.) Instead of pulling away from his children and their problems, Walter needs to become more closely involved in discipline. He needs to organize a method of setting and enforcing limits with the kinds of consequences presented in this three-step discipline program of discipline.

Amy the Appeaser

Amy wants peace at any cost. Her approach to discipline is very permissive because she tries to avoid any unpleasant confrontation with her child and can't stand the thought of being embarrassed in public by disruptive behavior. So she gives her daughter, Sara, anything she wants just to keep her quiet. She has become her child's slave.

Amy knows what's right and wrong, and so she will tell her daughter, "You can't have a cookie before dinner." Her daughter, however, knows that if she makes some noise, her mom will give in. And so she will go into her foot-stamping routine and cry, "I want a cookie now!" To keep peace, Amy will hand her a cookie and wistfully sigh to her visitor, "Sarah just insists on having her own way. I don't know what to do with her."

In this house, little Sara has come up with an equation that reduces discipline to this simple formula:

"Mom says no + Sara stamps her feet and yells =
Mom says yes"

Remedy: Amy needs to take charge of herself and her child. It is not Sara's fault that she acts so demanding; Amy has taught her that to get her own way, all she has to do is make some noise. Amy has created a "spoiled brat." It's time to teach Sara that she cannot always have her own way, that there are some rules that must be followed, that behaving, even when you don't want to, is a part of growing up. The three-step program will help Amy to do this. Sara, of course, will resist limit setting, and she will become enraged when Amy tries to enforce consequences, but if Amy stands firm, with Sara's best intentions at heart, she will soon find that Sara will get used to the idea that she is no longer in charge. (See page 132.)

Ivan the Intimidator

Ivan rules with the proverbial iron hand. He dominates his children the way a drill sergeant controls his troops: He insists on instant obedience; he bellows; he hits; he pushes, and he ridicules. He has no patience for questions, discussions, or reasons. His entire method of discipline relies on one sentence: "Do it now because I said so!" He bullies and intimidates his children, yet he holds himself up as a model parent to his neighbors when their children talk back or act sassy. "My kids would never do that," he gloats. "They know better."

Ivan's children do obey him, and it looks as if he knows what he's doing, but most likely, Ivan doesn't realize what he's doing to his children's emotional health. Children who are disciplined by brute intimidation often become withdrawn and fearful of authority figures. They learn to doubt their own feelings because they are expected to love this person who treats them so cruelly. Because these children seldom have the chance to make risky decisions or mistakes without suffering severe consequences, they never develop confidence in their own competence or ability to make judgments.

Ivan's method of discipline will work only as long as his children let it. When they grow older, they may look for ways to escape his wrath through drugs, alcohol, sex, running away, or suicide. Or they may stand up to him and refuse to listen regardless of what he does to them. Either way, Ivan's method of control will no longer be effective.

Remedy: Unfortunately, parents like Ivan believe that they are doing what is best for their children and because their children may initially act well-behaved, they see no reason to change.

If Ivan should realize that his method of discipline is too harsh (or if his spouse can convince him), he can try to soften his reaction to negative behaviors by using the three-step discipline. Most parents like Ivan, however, need professional counseling to help them see discipline as a gradual teaching process, rather than a command for blind obedience.

Pass-the-Buck Brenda

Brenda believes that her son needs to be disciplined, but she wants someone else to do it. When five-year-old Gary misbehaves, she is quick to tell him, "Wait 'till your father gets home. Boy, you're gonna get it." When

Greg clowns around too much, she warns him, "If your teacher sees you acting like that, she's going to be angry." And when December comes around, Brenda has twenty-four days to say, "I hope Santa is watching you act like that. He knows when you're being bad." Brenda has relinquished her ability to control her child. She is hoping that all these other people will be able to influence his behavior.

Remedy: Brenda must memorize and use this important rule of discipline: "Negative behaviors must be dealt *when they happen.* A young child often does not relate a delayed consequence to an earlier misdeed." (See page 110.) When Brenda sees her son misbehaving, *she* must be the one to deal with the problem. Passing the buck is unfair to her child, since it does not teach him how to behave. It is also unfair to the people to whom she passes the responsibility. It puts them in the position of having to punish an act that they did not see and know nothing about.

Procrastinating Pete

Pete knows how to discipline. He has set household rules; he has stated the consequences of breaking those rules, and he carries through on their enforcement. Pete's problem is his sense of timing:

- When Pete's eight-year-old daughter broke a rule by coming home late for supper, he decided to let it slide because he had company. Later, at bedtime, he gave her a scolding.
- When Pete's three-year-old threw a tantrum in the grocery store, he growled through clenched teeth, "You're going right to the time-out chair when we get home."
- When Pete's five-year-old took his tools out of the shed without asking, Pete looked up from his computer and said, "When I finish this project, you're going to be punished."

Remedy: Pete has to make himself stop whatever he's doing and take time to enforce his rules. And he has to learn how to discipline in front of other people. The moment his daughter walked in late, he should have left his company for a few minutes to scold her in another room. In the supermarket, Pete should have left his grocery cart, picked up his screaming child, and found an out-of-the-way place (the car, the stairs, the sidewalk) to impose an immediate time-out. And he should have left his computer project the moment he saw his son with the tools. (See page 110.)

Patty Perfectionist

Patty has unrealistic expectations of her child's ability to follow rules. She has no patience for the normal childhood learning process, which includes forgetfulness and regression. Once a rule is set, she expects her daughter to follow it always. Therefore, if her child hangs up her coat on Monday, there is no excuse for not doing it again on Friday. She also has no tolerance for childish things like fooling around, making a mess, stepping in puddles, or touching food.

Sometimes Patty impresses her friends with her nononsense approach to discipline and her swift reaction to problems. However, if you've had the chance to consistently watch this method of discipline in action, you've also probably noticed that it puts a great deal of pressure on the child. In the long run, this kind of parental pressure is likely to leave a child feeling inept, insecure, and angry at you.

Remedy: First, Patty needs a lesson in the developmental stages of childhood (see Appendix A, page 204). This information will help her set limits that her daughter will have the ability to meet, and it will help her understand that forgetfulness and regression are to be expected when children are learning new things. With the probability of regression in mind, Pat also should give her daughter a warning before she jumps right to punishment. This will remind her daughter of the rule and give her a chance to behave. (See page 103.) Children need guidance and help to attain socially acceptable behaviors. Parents who expect perfection in children will be continually disappointed and the children will become disappointed in themselves.

Greg the Guilt-tripper

Greg doesn't see good behavior as a learned skill that results from setting basic household rules. He sees it as repayment for all the things he does for his children. When they do not behave, he feels it is a personal attack on him. Greg disciplines with statements like these:

"How could you lie to me, after all I've done for you?"

"I can't believe you broke that toy, when you know I went out of my way to get it for you."

"I've spent the last hour playing with you, and now you repay me by talking fresh?"

"You keep this up and you're going to give me an ulcer."

Remedy: If Greg is saying these things because he uses guilt as his primary disciplinary strategy, he should make a conscious effort to develop other approaches. Intense guilt does not motivate children to learn right from wrong, and it does not foster self-discipline or moral growth. Instead, children who are raised with excessive doses of guilt often grow up with a very low level of self-esteem.

Greg also needs to learn more about his children's intellectual and moral development. Children are not as devious, cunning, plotting, or vindictive as parents like Greg think. Their actions are most often without ulterior motives. (See Appendix A, page 204.) They do not misbehave because they are ungrateful or because they want to drive their parents to an early grave. They "misbehave" because they have not yet learned the rules that help them adjust their behavior in ways that are acceptable to society.

Threatening Thelma

Thelma tries to get her son to behave by describing in graphic detail the horrible things she will do to him if he doesn't obey her. Throughout the day she barks out one threat after another:

"You do that again and I'll break every bone in your body."

"You won't think it's so funny when you're wiping blood off your face."

"If you talk to me like that one more time, I'm gonna wrap your tongue around your neck and tie it like a bow tie."

Of course Thelma doesn't mean any of these things, and of course her son knows it. Thelma's threats give him no motivation or reason to behave.

Remedy: Thelma has to learn to state realistic warnings that she can and will follow through on. "If you talk like that to me one more time, you cannot go to Andy's party this afternoon." This is an effective way to change negative behaviors. Threatening wild, unenforceable consequences doesn't do a thing. Children will continue to misbehave as they mumble under their breath. "Yeah, sure." (See "Stating a Warning," page 103.)

Stan the Storm Trooper

Stan is basically an easy-going kind of guy. He spends lots of time with his two boys every weekend. He tries to understand their bouts of silliness and sibling spats. As the day moves along he tries to deal with their negative behaviors by first ignoring them, then by reasoning with his boys, and then by bribing them. Then around seven o'clock at night, all of Stan's patience and tolerance is gone. During all the hours of misbehaving, his anger has been building up and it now begins to overflow. When the boys come running to him with yet another argument—BAM! Without warning, Stan explodes. He's had it! He yells; he bellows; he hits; he slams doors; he sends them both to bed; and he feels awful.

Remedy: Stan can't let his boys get away with misbehaving all day until they push him over the edge. Earlier in the day, when Timmy first spit on Carl, Stan should have set a limit that prohibited fighting. (See page 63.) During the rest of the day, Stan should have enforced the promised penalty each time one of them started a spat (page 105) and complimented and rewarded them when they played nicely (page 94). By not doing anything forceful and immediate about the boys' fighting over an eight-hour period, Stan gave his sons the message that it was okay. Imagine how surprised they were to find that at 7:05 P.M. it wasn't okay anymore. Many parents, like Stan, explode at the end of the day because they "just can't take it anymore." If a behavior is unacceptable in the evening, it was probably also unacceptable in the morning and afternoon. And that's when it should be stopped.

Contradicting Cathy

Cathy has established a program of discipline in which she sets rules and immediately enforces them. In punishing her daughter, Lauren, however, she sometimes does the very things that she tells Lauren not to do. These mixed messages confuse Lauren, and they make it difficult for her to believe that her actions are really wrong.

You have heard Cathy in the supermarket when she yells down the aisle at the top of her voice, "Lauren, stop yelling!" You've seen her at the playground when she hits Lauren's hands and says, "Don't you ever hit anyone. That's not nice." Cathy is also the one who makes fun of people, and then tells Lauren to be kind and considerate to others. Cathy lies for her husband ("Bob won't be at work today because he's sick") and then tells Lauren she must never lie.

Remedy: The "Do as I say, not as I do" method of child-rearing has never been an effective way to teach children what's right and wrong. This is especially so when the spoken message ("don't hit") is exactly opposite the parent's actions (smack). Cathy can't use aggressive tactics to teach her child to be nonviolent. She can't teach her not to yell by yelling at her. Cathy has to model the behavior she wants her child to adopt. (See page 54.)

Tired Tim

Tim wants his children to behave, and when he's with them he knows that he should be setting and enforcing rules. But most often his discipline tactics only serve to confuse his children. "I know I should be more consistent in the way I discipline my kids," says Tim, "but most of the time I'm just too tired to keep after them. Either I ignore the poor behavior, or I snap at the slightest thing."

Remedy: Tim is certainly not alone in his problem. In today's hurried world, many parents who try to balance a busy household and active, into-everything children often become lax in their approach to discipline. Good discipline does take time, patience, and fortitude, but just as you feed and clothe your child each day, even when you're tired, so should you teach him how to behave. In the long run, the effort will be worthwhile because a well-behaved child lessens the drain on your daily energy supply.

When tiredness is caused by mild depression, or when stressful life situations such as a death in the family, a divorce, or an illness inhibit your ability to effectively discipline your child, it's probably not a good idea to start a new program of discipline. Wait until the tension eases and you have more mental strength to devote to your child. In the meantime, you and your child will probably feel a lot better if you use some of the suggestions presented in Chapter Two. This information will help you build a strong, positive family relationship that can withstand the stress you're now experiencing.

Camille the Chameleon

Camille changes her method of rule enforcement to match her mood. Sometimes she is the intimidator. Sometimes she is the ostrich. And other times she is a screamer. Her kids don't know what to expect from one moment to the next, and so, in general, they do whatever they please hoping it's at the time when Mom won't care.

Remedy: No parent is totally consistent in his or her disciplining tactics day in and day out. We all bend the rules some days, and we all become more demanding on others. But the foundation of disciplinary expectations should remain intact even when swayed a bit. Camille, however, swings from being totally permissive one moment to being very strict the next. In one week's time, a parent like Camille may cover most of the discipline "strategies" presented in this chapter.

Camille needs to learn the importance of consistency. (See page 53.) No new skill can be effectively learned if the teacher is inconsistent and unpredictable in his approach. If Camille cannot make herself stick to an effective disciplinary method like the three-step program, she should seek professional help from her pediatrician or a school, community, or private psychologist.

Chapter 10
Children with Problems

When your child misbehaves, take heart in knowing that somewhere at that very moment, some other child is doing the exact same thing. The vast majority of discipline problems are common ones. This chapter lists (in alphabetical order) thirty such problems; it describes children who are struggling with them; and it explains how you can use the three-step program of discipline to resolve them. It also includes page references back to the three-step program of discipline if you need to refresh your memory.

As you use this quick reference to handle your discipline problems, remember: Without exception, the key to effectively controlling the problem areas listed below is to choose a suggested plan of action and then use it consistently and persistently.

SPECIFIC MISBEHAVIORS

Automobile Rides

Kenny doesn't like to be confined. He always argues and cries when his parents insist that he put on his seatbelt in the car. If his parents manage to get the buckle secured, Kenny will open it as soon as his mom or dad is busy driving the car. "This is a dangerous situation that I can't just ignore," says his dad. "But it's such a battle even to take a short drive to the store for a quart of milk that I sometimes give up and let him ride without the belt."

REMEDY

Set a Limit
"You must have your seatbelt buckled when you are in the car because that will keep you safe from harm if we have an accident."

Emphasize the Positive

- Praise your child each time he wears the seatbelt.
- Set a good example by buckling up your own belt.
- Use Grandma's Rule (page 86): "If you buckle your seatbelt now, you will be allowed to go out and play this afternoon."

Impose a Penalty for Disobedience
Choose one.

- Explain to your child that the car doesn't move unless the seatbelt is buckled (loss of a privilege, page 118). Bring a book or magazine to read while you wait for your child to agree. If your child unbuckles while you're driving, pull the car off the road and wait for him to rebuckle. Don't argue; this isn't negotiable. If it's a realistic option, tell your child that if he refuses to use the seatbelt, he cannot ride in your car: "Buckle the belt or stay home."
- If necessary, buckle your child's seatbelt for him. If someone else is driving, you can hold your hand over the buckle so he can't undo it (physical assistance, page 128).

Tips

The most common behavior problems that parents face while traveling with children are those that distract them from the job of driving. These include clowning around, fighting, and whining. If you have this kind of problem while riding in the car, treat each behavior as you would if it were happening at home: Before you start the car, set the limits. If your children break the rules while you're driving, pull the car over and impose one of the penalties suggested under the specific headings of "sibling fights," "whining," or whichever behavior your children are engaging in.

Back Talk

When Anne's parents ask her to do something (clean her room or feed the dog, for example), she responds with verbal tantrums. She argues, yells, or angrily debates: "No. I won't." "I'm too busy right now." "Sharon's parents don't make her do that." "Leave me alone." This kind of back talk has become so persistent and predictable that her parents find themselves avoiding discipline situations just to avoid the loud confrontation they know will follow. "I can't stand Anne's constant back talk!" complains her mother. "And I know that when I yell right back at her I'm only aggravating the situation, but it makes me so angry when she talks like that."

REMEDY

Set a Limit

"You can always explain your side of a story by talking in a calm manner. But in this house, we don't scream, swear, or yell back at people."

Emphasize the Positive

- Show appreciation when your child listens without talking back.

- Set a good example by responding to your child's questions in a calm tone of voice so you don't sound as if you're jumping on the "back talk bandwagon."
- Permit normal mumbling and grumbling.

Impose a Penalty for Disobedience
Tell your child that if he talks back to you (choose one):

- He'll have to go to the time-out chair until he's quiet and ready to do what you ask without arguing (time-out, page 122).
- You will ignore him until he can quiet himself down and do as he is told (ignoring, page 97).
- He will lose one minute of TV time for every minute he continues to talk back (loss of a privilege, page 118).

Bad Language

Helen is furious every time she hears her eight-year-old son, Ralph, cursing and swearing at his friend as they argue in the backyard. She is tired of telling him not to talk like that. For the past few months, he had constantly embarrassed and angered her with his use of foul language. Today's outburst was the last straw. She would not have him screaming those "dirty" words all over the neighborhood anymore.

REMEDY

Set a Limit
"People in this family do not use foul language. You may not talk like that because it shows disrespect to the people you say it to, it embarrasses and angers your parents, and because it gives people a negative impression of you. This includes words like shit, fuck, damn, piss, and asshole."

Emphasize the Positive

- Tell your child that for each day he does not use bad language, he will get a token chip. Let him trade seven of those chips for a pizza party with two of his friends (rewards, page 86).
- Compliment him when you notice he has not used bad language in a situation where he might have.
- Set a good example by eliminating vulgar words from your own vocabulary.

Impose a Penalty for Disobedience

Tell your child that if he uses bad language again (choose one):

- He will go to the time-out chair for eight minutes (time-out, page 122).
- He will be scolded (brief scoldings, page 119).
- He will be ignored (ignoring, page 97). This method is appropriate only if you feel your child is using bad language simply to get your attention or to anger you.
- He will pay a fine of twenty-five cents each time he uses bad language. This will be taken out of his allowance (loss of a possession, page 118).

Tips

You can sometimes control bad language by showing your child how to express his anger in acceptable ways, such as coming right out and saying what's bothering him: "I can't stand it when you borrow my things and don't put them back."

Children under the age of four generally use profanity to experiment with new words and to see what kind of reaction they'll get from their parents. Older children may begin to use these words to express their anger, or to impress their friends, or to defy or shock their parents. Try to determine why your child is using bad language; it will help you decide how to handle it.

Bedtime Problems

Problem 1: Refusing to Go to Bed

Bedtime at the Stone household is not a time for warm snuggles and sweet good-night kisses. It is a time for pleading, and crying, and trying to convince three-year-old Josh that he must go to bed. A typical night begins like this:

"I'm not tired," yells Josh.

"You need your sleep. Now get into bed," yells his dad.

"Please?"

"No!"

"Just five more minutes?"

"All right, but then right to bed."

REMEDY

Set an Impersonal Limit (page 63):

"When the clock says eight o'clock, it's time for you to go to bed."

Emphasize the Positive

- Tell your child that if he goes to bed right away, without any crying or arguing, he will get a star on his star chart. When he get four stars, you'll take him to see the movie he wants to see (sample chart, page 88).
- Praise your child when he goes to bed without arguing.

Impose Penalties for Disobedience

If your child continues to cry or argue when it's time for bed, tell him that you will carry him to his room and then ignore his crying (physical assistance, page 128, ignoring, page 97).

Tips

- Establish a consistent bedtime and wake-up routine. This will help your child be physically ready for sleep at the same hour every night.

- The hour before bedtime should be a calm and relaxing time, without rough or exciting play. The routine at bedtime should involve about twenty minutes alone with one parent who provides warmth and comfort.
- Consider your child's changing sleep needs. As children grow their need for sleep changes. You may be able to avoid bedtime battles by structuring your child's schedule so that he is sleepy at bedtime. This sometimes means eliminating the afternoon nap, or moving it to a time earlier in the day. It may also mean moving the bedtime up to a later hour.
- Give your child a five-minute warning before it's time for bed.

Problem 2: Leaving the Bed During the Night

Five-year-old Kerry goes to bed without a problem every night at eight o'clock. But Kerry's parents know that they'll see her again before the morning. Kerry gets out of her bed and goes into her parents' room every night to ask for a glass of water, or assistance in going to the bathroom, or to complain of bad dreams, or to climb into their bed because she's lonely.

Kerry's parents want her to stay in her own bed because they know she needs her sleep—and they need their sleep, too. But no matter how many times they send her back to bed, she pops back up again. They've found that the only way to get any sleep is to let her into their bed.

REMEDY

Set a Limit
"You cannot come into our bedroom and wake us up. You need your sleep and we need ours."

Emphasize the Positive

- Tell your child that if he doesn't wake up during the night, you will let him watch his favorite video tape in the morning.
- Praise him in the morning when he stays in bed all night.
- Leave the bathroom light on, and put a glass of water on the night table so if your child really does need them in the night he can help himself without waking you.

Impose Penalties for Disobedience

Tell your child if he does wake you, you will lead him back to his room (physical assistance, page 128). Also tell him if he cries, you will close the door (loss of a privilege, page 118) so you can't hear him (ignoring, page 97). And it will be opened only when he stops crying.

Tips

- Return your child to his bed within ten to fifteen seconds after he gets up.
- Promptly return the child to his bed *every* time he gets up.

Other Bedtime Problems

Some children resist going to bed or get out of bed at night because you have taught them to need your comfort to go to sleep, or because they are afraid of the dark, or because they suffer separation anxieties at bedtime (especially those eighteen months to four years old), or because they are affected by nightmares or night terrors. These are not discipline problems that can be solved with the three-step program of discipline. They are sleep disturbances that need special handling. To find out how to handle these situations you can talk to your pediatrician, contact a child psychologist, or read *Teach Your Baby to Sleep Through the Night* by Dr. Charles Schaefer and Dr. Michael Petronko.

Biting

Two-year-old Kyle is known as the neighborhood biter. He bites big boys, little girls, old men, tiny babies, mothers, fathers, friends, foes, and even animals. Sometimes he bites if someone angered him, other times he bites in self-defense, but still other times he bites for no apparent reason at all. His parents are now at the point where they stand next to him whenever he's within attack range of another person, so they can run interference. Kyle doesn't seem to understand that biting hurts other people. His uncle thinks someone should bite Kyle so he'll learn how it feels.

REMEDY

Set a Limit
"People are not for biting because it hurts them and they don't like it."

Emphasize the Positive

- Offer your child a reward (page 84) like an ice cream cone if he can play with his friend without biting.
- Praise your child when you see him interact with other people without biting.
- Show your child alternate ways to express his anger when biting is the result of confrontation.

Impose a Penalty for Disobedience

- Give your child a brief scolding every time he bites someone (page 119). This will remind him that you disapprove, tell him why, and offer him an alternative.
- Whenever you see your child bite someone else, send him immediately to the time-out chair (page 122).
- Have your child right the wrong (page 115) by patting the area of the bite for thirty seconds and apologizing ten times after each bite. If you catch your

child attempting to bite, have him apologize twenty times.

- You might also control biting if you use a logical consequence that takes away the privilege of play, such as: "If you bite Nancy I will take you home and you will not be allowed to play with her for the rest of the day." (loss of a privilege, page 118).

Tips

- Impose the promised consequence promptly *every time* your child bites (page 110).
- Avoid aggressive punishments. Do not hit your child. This only teaches him that aggression is an acceptable way to interact with other people (page 129).

Climbing (trees, fences, tables, etc.)

Four-year-old Gina acts as if she is in training to scale Mount Everest; she loves to climb. But her parents realize that Gina could seriously hurt herself when she tries to climb the backyard trees and fences, because her motor coordination skills are not yet fine-tuned. No matter how many times they tell her she may not climb, she runs right back out and does it again.

REMEDY

Set a Limit
"You may not climb the trees or the fences in our backyard because you may fall and get seriously hurt."

Emphasize the Positive

- If your child loves to climb, take him to a park where he can spend the afternoon on a jungle gym or climbing bars under your close supervision.
- Praise play activities that do not involve climbing.
- Show your child alternate play activities.

Impose a Penalty for Disobedience

When you see your child climbing in places where he is not allowed, send him to the time-out chair (page 123).

Clowning

Three-year-old Joey loves to giggle and dance around, and make funny faces. There are times, however, when this silly behavior drives his parents mad. "Sometimes it's just impossible to get him dressed, or to wash his face, or even to get him to sit still long enough for a kiss good-bye," sighs Joey's dad. "I hate yelling at him when all he's really doing is being a kid and having fun, but there are times he has to stop it and do what I ask him."

REMEDY

Set a Limit

"You can play, and laugh, and have fun, but you must stop clowning around when I need you to pay attention to me and hear what I'm saying."

Emphasize the Positive

- Show your child (especially through your own actions) other ways in which humor can be expressed, like jokes, cartoons, pictures, stories, (page 16).
- Praise your child's efforts to control his clowning around and use humor appropriately.
- Find other outlets, such as sports, clubs, dance lessons, where your child's need to be the center of attention can be accommodated.

Impose a Penalty for Disobedience

- If you feel your child's clowning around is an attempt to gain your attention, ignore it (page 97).
- If you feel your child's silliness has become an out-of-control habit, send him to the time-out chair as soon as he begins to act up (time-out, page 122).

Tips

Permit as much silliness as you can stand. Most children who go through this stage soon grow out of it (tolerating, page 51).

Sometimes children will attempt to supply comic relief in homes where there are family tensions. If your child is disruptive in his silliness, and at the same time you are having marital or personal problems, you may be able to control his clowning by resolving your own conflicts (page 00).

Other children will use clowning as a way to get more attention from you, especially when there is a new baby in the house. Although ignoring is an appropriate technique when your child is acting silly because he wants to get you off the phone, it is not the best approach if the silliness is a cry from a lonely child. In this case, schedule more quality time with your child (page 25), give him a few extra hugs and kisses (page 22), and watch the silliness subside.

Chores

Seven-year-old Melissa won't help out around the house. Each day Melissa is supposed to fold her pajamas and put them away, walk the dog after school, and before bed, lay out her school clothes for the following morning. Every day Melissa refuses. "I know I should make Melissa do her chores," says her mom, "but she'll argue with me for an hour and the chores still won't get done. So it's much easier and faster if I do them myself."

REMEDY

Set a Limit

"Everyone in this family helps out around the house. You have three chores to do every day: Fold and put away your pajamas before breakfast; walk the dog when you get home from school; get your clothes ready each night for the next morning. I've written them down and taped them on the refrigerator so you won't forget what they are."

Emphasize the Positive

- Use the star chart (page 88). Tell your child, "Every time you do a chore, you can put a star on the list that's on the fridge. When you have done all your chores for three days in a row, you can buy a new sweater to wear to school."
- Praise your child every time a chore is done.
- Do your own chores without complaining (page 54).

Impose a Penalty for Disobedience

Tell your child the consequence of not doing each chore:

- "If you do not fold and put away your pajamas, you will be scolded, and I will take your hands and help you do it." (scolding, page 119; physical assistance, page 128).
- "If you do not walk the dog, you can not go out to play in the afternoon" (loss of a privilege, page 118; Grandma's rule, page 86).
- "If you do not lay out your clothes at night, you will be rushed putting together an outfit in the morning, but that will be your choice." (learning the hard way, page 101).

Tips

- Be realistic in your expectations. Do not give your child too many chores or ones that are too difficult to do. If he feels overwhelmed, he won't do any of them.
- Don't give a young child too many directives. Children younger than five can't remember more than three instructions at a time.

Cruelty to Pets

Three-year-old Larry is treating his pets (a dog and two cats) very cruelly. He has tied the cats together with rope; he has put a paper bag over the dog's head so she couldn't see; he has hit them with his baseball bat, yelled at them, and chased them around the yard threatening to kill. "The more I yell at Larry for doing these awful things to his pets," says Larry's mom, "the more he does them."

REMEDY

Set a Limit

"You cannot do anything to your pets that will hurt them. This includes hitting, yelling, tying them up, or anything else that you would not like someone to do to you. Animals have feelings just like you and these things hurt them."

Emphasize the Positive

- Praise your child when he treats his pets kindly.
- Model a kind and caring attitude toward animals.
- Show your child acceptable ways to play with his pet.
- Offer him a reward for playing nicely with his pet, like a new toy for the pet, or a new dog coat, or a new pet.

Impose a Penalty for Disobedience

Tell your child, "If you to hurt your pets again (choose one):

- I will give the animals away to someone who will care for them properly" (learning the hard way, page 101). (Don't state this consequence unless you are ready to follow through and do it.)
- You will be scolded and sent to your time-out chair" (brief scoldings, page 119; time-out, page 122).
- You will no longer be allowed to play with your pets for the rest of the day" (loss of a privilege, page 118).

Tips

Children younger than four years may see animals as play things and treat them in the same rough manner they do their toys. This, of course, can be painful for the pet. If your child tends to do this, encourage kindness and gentle care through example and explanation, but also try not to leave your child alone with the animal.

A child over the age of three who persistently abuses animals may need professional counseling. If it is an aggressive inclination rather than a lack of empathy, it should be addressed early to find its cause and to help the child and his family resolve the problem before it becomes deep-seated.

Destroying Property

It seems as if Gail spends most of her day just looking for things to break, rip, and ruin. Her parents marvel that one little girl can destroy so many things. Gail can rip apart a complete novel borrowed from the library faster than her mom can dash across the room to save it. When visiting, she can break fine china and crystal before her dad even has his coat off. There isn't a wall in their home that hasn't been "autographed" by Gail's creative mark, and there isn't a toy in Gail's room that hasn't been examined to pieces. Gail's parents feel that almost all this destruction is done in the name of curiosity and creativity rather than a desire to destroy, but they still want it to stop.

REMEDY

Set a Limit

Set a specific limit for each problem behavior. "Don't destroy things" is too vague.

Limit 1: "Books are not for ripping; they are for reading."

Emphasize the Positive

- Offer your child a reward: "If you do not rip any books this week, I will buy a new book on Saturday" (rewards, page 86). (For children under the age of four, set a new limit each day. "Saturday" has no meaning.)
- Praise your child when he reads a book without ripping it.
- Treat your own and his books with care.
- Have a daily ten-minute "demolition" time when your child can destroy old books and magazines you provide for this purpose. Explain that these are the *only* books he's allowed to destroy.

Impose a Penalty for Disobedience
Tell your child, "If you do rip a book [choose one]:

- You will tape back together every page you rip" (right the wrong, page 115). Help younger children complete this task.
- I will take away all of your books for the rest of the day" (loss of possessions, page 118).
- You will use your allowance money to replace whatever you destroy" (right the wrong, page 115).

Limit 2: "Walls are not for drawing on."

Emphasize the Positive

- Praise your child when he draws on paper.
- Bring your child to an art show and show him all the pictures on "paper."

Impose a Penalty for Disobedience
Tell your child, "If you draw on any walls this week, [choose one]:

- I will take away your crayons for the rest of the day" (loss of a possession, page 118).

- You will be scolded and sent to the time-out chair" (brief scolding, page 119; time-out, page 122). This is only appropriate if you catch your child in the act.
- You will scrub the wall clean" (right the wrong, page 115).

Tips

- Redirect your child to acceptable creative activities like paints, coloring books, and old magazines that can be ripped.
- Show care for other people's and your own possessions.
- Many destructive behaviors can be eliminated through preventive tactics such as reorganizing your home environment so that breakables are put away (page 48); keeping scissors, crayons, and pens out of reach until you're ready to supervise their use; buying your child toys that are tough and have take-apart pieces; postponing or rescheduling visits to houses where there are many breakable objects within easy reach (page 51).

Disobedience

"You never mind me! I told you to turn off the TV and come to the kitchen for dinner." Tina heard her dad tell her what to do; she just doesn't listen to him anymore. She has tuned out the sound of his requests, commands, suggestions, and advice. If your dad says, "Tina, your friend is at the door," Tina's ears would work just fine. "I know Tina hears me," says her dad. "How can I make her follow my directions?"

REMEDY

Set a Limit
"When I tell you to do something, I want you to give me your full attention, and do what I say to do."

Emphasize the Positive

- Offer a reward for obedience:
  "When you mind me, I will give you a star on this good-behavior chart. When you get five stars, I'll rent a video movie for you" (sample chart, page 88).
- Use the body language techniques described on page 74–76. It is difficult for a child to ignore a parents who stands within three feet, squats to his level, looks him in the eye, says his first name, talks directly to him, and asks for a response.
- Praise your child when he does comply.
- Set a good example by listening with full attention, and complying (if possible) with requests your child asks of you.

Impose a Penalty for Disobedience

Tell your child, "If you do not mind me [choose one]:

- I will immediately interrupt what you're doing and scold you" (brief scolding, page 119).
- You will not be allowed to watch TV tonight." (loss of a privilege, page 118).
- You will go to the time-out chair" (time-out, page 122).

Tips

Limit the number of directives you give at one time. Most children under the age of five have great difficulty following through on more than three directives: "Turn off the TV; call your brother; wash your hands and come and eat," is too many things to remember. Your child may therefore opt to do nothing.

Disrespect for Adults

Eight-year-old Dottie shows no respect for her elders. She treats them as if they are the kids next door whom she can talk back to and make wise-cracks to. Her parents try to explain to Dottie that it is a show of good manners to treat adults with respect, but Dottie usually responds only with some wise remark that is disrespectful to them. "I was so embarrassed this morning," her mom confided to a friend. "A woman I work with dropped by to say, 'Hello,' and when she told Dottie that she looked a lot like me, Dottie laughed and said, 'Oh yeah? Well, I think you look like Frankenstein.' "

REMEDY

Set a Limit
"You must show respect to adults. You cannot use fresh and smart-alecky remarks when you talk to them."

Emphasize the Positive

- Praise your child when he treats adults with respect. Tell him, "I'm very proud of the way you speak to my friends."
- Set a good example by speaking with respect to your friends, your spouse, and your child.
- Avoid telling "behind-the-back" stories that show disrespect to people.

Impose a Penalty for Disobedience
Tell your child, "If you don't show my guests the proper respect [choose one]:

- You will be scolded and sent out of the room" (brief scolding, page 119; loss of a privilege, page 118).
- You will not be allowed to have your friends in this house at any time tomorrow" (loss of a privilege, page 118).
- You will apologize to and do something nice for anyone you offend" (right the wrong, page 115).

Tips
Before the age of five, children may have difficulty understanding that the way one speaks to an adult is sometimes different than the way one speaks to a friend. You can better foster this understanding by treating

your child and others with respect so your child has proper behavior to mimic. Respect is better taught through example and encouragement than through punishment.

Eating Problems

Problem 1: Refusal to Eat

It seems as if Jimmy woke up one morning and decided never to eat again. Her parents first worried that he was ill. When the doctor ruled out poor health, they thought he was just being stubborn. "Food has become the focus of our entire day," says his mother. "We fight at all three meals. All he does is sit there and stare at his food. I've even tried one of my mother's tricks by giving him the same plate of cold food all day long. I'm angry at him for being so stubborn, and I'm also worried about his health."

REMEDY

Set a Limit

"You must sit at the table with me for twenty minutes when it's time to eat." (You can't force a child to swallow food, but you can make him give up his other activities and sit still long enough to eat if he's hungry.)

Emphasize the Positive

- Praise your child when he eats good foods.
- Give him a choice of foods that he likes to eat and prepare them in an attractive way.
- Set a good example by eating three meals a day. If you skip meals your child will learn that eating is not important.

Impose a Penalty for Disobedience

Tell your child, "If you don't eat your carrots, (choose one):

- You can't have any dessert" (loss of a privilege, page 118).

- You will soon be hungry, but you cannot have anything else to eat until the next mealtime." (learning the hard way, pp. 101)

Tips

Do not beg, argue, or give undue attention to eating. This will make eating a power game rather than a natural daily activity.

Most children go through phases when they do not want to eat. Sometimes they don't feel well; other times they're too busy exploring to take time out for chewing; sometimes they're just not hungry. Whatever the reason, if your child is physically active and alert, he is probably getting enough to eat.

If an adolescent child refuses to eat over a long period of time, this should be discussed with your family doctor. Sometimes in a concerted effort to lose weight, children (especially girls) may develop a life-threatening condition called anorexia nervosa.

Problem 2: Throwing Food

Randy's creative playtime extended right into mealtime. He squished, flipped, and threw his food over the table and across the room. Day after day, meal after meal, Randy disgusted his parents with these antics. Eating in restaurants or at friends' houses always ended in embarrassing outbursts of anger. Almost all meals ended in the same note: "This place looks like a pigpen!"

REMEDY

Set a Limit

"Food is for eating; not for throwing." (Set this limit well in advance of mealtime.)

Emphasize the Positive

- Praise your child when he eats without throwing.
- Have play tea parties and picnics where your child can teach proper table manners to his dolls and stuffed animals.
- Don't pick at your own food.

Impose a Penalty for Disobedience
Tell your child, "If you throw your food again (choose one):

- You will be scolded and sent to the time-out chair" (brief scolding, page 119; time-out, page 122).
- You will have to clean up the mess all by yourself" (right a wrong, page 115).

Tips

- Prepare foods that your child likes to eat.
- Take his plate away from the table when he's finished.
- Expect a certain amount of messiness when your child eats. Penalties are appropriate only when the mess is exaggerated and intentional.

Hitting

See "Biting," page 166. This same limit and consequence are appropriate for many aggressive acts including hitting, pinching, and pushing others. Also see page 127 for a detailed look at how one mother used time-out to stop her two-year-old from hitting other children.

Interrupting

Leslie wants all of her parents' attention all the time. If her mom or dad tries to watch TV, read the newspaper, or talk on the phone, Leslie will instantly need help, or a drink, or will have important questions that must be answered. "I give Leslie plenty of attention all day long," says her mom. "But I really feel that I need just a few minutes alone each day, even if it's just to go to the bathroom. If I stop to talk to a friend, or if the phone rings, she actually panics in her need to regain my attention. I think this is getting out of hand."

REMEDY

Set a Limit
Set a specific limit for each problem behavior. "Don't interrupt me when I'm busy" is too vague. "Do not talk to me while I'm talking on the phone because I can't hear what the other person is saying."

Emphasize the Positive

- Praise your child when he is quiet and waits for your attention.
- Distract your child with special toys before you begin your conversation.
- Set a good example by not interrupting other people.
- Offer a reward such as, "If you play alone for five minutes while I'm on the phone, I will then play a special game with you" (rewards, page 89).

Impose a Penalty for Disobedience
Tell your child, "If you leave the play area before the five minute timer rings [choose 1]:

- I will continue to do what I'm doing and completely ignore you until the five minutes are up" (ignoring, page 00).
- I will send you to the time-out chair until the five minutes are up" (time-out, page 122). Don't wait until you finish your phone call. Excuse yourself for a moment, put your child in time-out, and then return to your conversation.

Tips

- You can increase the amount of time you want your child to leave you alone as he gets older and more accustomed to giving you some privacy, but don't expect him to stay away for much longer than fifteen minutes.
- Use a kitchen timer to mark when your child may expect your full attention again.

Leaving the House or Yard Without Permission

Harry's mom calls him a gypsy. "Every time I turn around, he's gone. I don't know where he thinks he's going, but his goal each day is to get out of this house and wander around the streets."

REMEDY

Set a Limit
"You cannot go outside by yourself because you may get lost or hurt."

Emphasize the Positive

- Offer a reward. Tell your child, "If you stay inside until I've finished the housework, you can take me for a long walk all around town."
- Praise your child when he waits for you to take him out.
- When you're too busy to supervise his every move, try to be sure he has something (toys, puzzles) to keep him occupied.

Impose a Penalty for Disobedience
Tell your child, "If you go out of this house by yourself, I will bring you back inside, and you will have to stay in for the rest of the day" (physical assistance, page 128; loss of a privilege, page 118).

Tips

- Keep your house doors firmly locked.
- Don't leave your child alone in the house or yard.

Leaving the premises unsupervised is a dangerous behavior. Since children under the age of five can't be trusted to stay where you put them, it would not be appropriate to set a limit and then feel they are safe. If your young child insists on wandering away, you must diligently use preventive tactics by keeping him in sight and locking the doors. Children five years and older can start to take on the responsibility of staying in a safe area, alone, but be sure they understand the rule about wandering away and the consequence for disobedience.

Lying

It is very difficult to discipline a child who lies. Children under the age of six "lie" because they have a rich imagination and the line between reality and fantasy is hard to define. Very often their "lies" are not intentional negative behaviors, but rather experiments in storytelling.

Children six years and older most often lie to avoid punishment. Excessive lying is usually caused by harsh or frequent punishments or a need to please adults with high expectations. Their lying, therefore, may be primarily a mechanism of self-defense rather than antisocial behavior. In this case both the child and the parents may need professional help to overcome this kind of lying, which has its roots in psychological needs rather than in lack of discipline.

Messiness

The same thought goes through Jim's mind every day when he comes home from work: "This place looks like a tornado hit it." His wife scurries around all day picking up one mess after another, but she never seems to keep up with the messes that Megan keeps making. "As fast as I can clean one mess," she says, "Megan has created two more. I've tried to get her to help me clean up a little, or at least slow down the messing process, but she just won't."

REMEDY

Set a Limit
"You can play with this toy, but you must put it away when you're finished."

Emphasize the Positive

- Offer a reward. Tell your child: "If you show me that you know how to take care of your toys by putting them away, I will buy you a new one."
- Use a star chart. Tell your child: "If you clean up your mess each night [specify which "mess"—crayons, toys, clothes] you will get a star on this cleanup chart. You can trade in six stars for a new toy." (Or whatever reward is appropriate. See page 88 for sample chart.)
- Give your child outlets for messy fun (digging in the dirt, playing with clay, finger-painting).
- Rather than forbid a mess, protect against it. Put down a drop cloth when your child is using paint or clay. Use a large bib when you serve a toddler spaghetti. Save old clothes to use for outdoor fun.
- Praise your child when he cleans up after himself.
- Set a good example by cleaning up after yourself.
- Involve your child in daily household chores to create an atmosphere of cooperation.

Impose a Penalty for Disobedience
Tell your child, "If you do not clean up your mess (choose one):

- No one will do it for you, and your things will get ruined" (learning the hard way, page 101).

- I will take your hands and 'help' you do it" (physical assistance, page 128).
- You will not be allowed to use these things tomorrow" (logical loss of privilege, page 118).
- You cannot go outside" (loss of a privilege, page 118).

Tips

- Expect your child to be reasonably messy.
- Be specific when it's time to clean up. Do not say, "Clean your room." Say, "Pick up the toys and clothing" (page 70).
- Leave humorous notes to remind your older child of your clean-up expectations.

Kids are messy. The use of discipline, therefore, is really a question of degree. How much messiness can you tolerate, and how much is too much to be ignored? The best approach to dealing with your child's mess is to use preventive tactics (old clothes, drop clothes, etc.), and to use limits when the mess causes an unhealthy or unsafe environment.

Name-calling

See "Bad Language," page 161. The limits and consequences that can control the use of vulgar language can also be applied to stop your child's habit of calling people names like, "dummy," "stupid," and "nerd." The best way, of course, to stop this kind of language is to make sure that you yourself never resort to name-calling.

Procrastination

Peter is slow to do things. His parents aren't sure if it's his nature or a technique he's developed specifically to drive them crazy. Either way, his procrastination causes daily family conflicts. "Getting Peter out the door in the morning is such a battle," says his mom. "He takes so long to get dressed, to get washed, to eat, even to put his coat on. If I didn't physically do everything for him, he'd never get to school."

REMEDY

Set a Limit
"You must be ready to leave the house every weekday morning at eight o'clock because you can't be late for school."

Emphasize the Positive

- Be sure to help your child meet this expectation by waking him up on time, setting his clothes out for him (or helping him set them out), and preparing breakfast.
- Praise your child when he is ready on time.
- Point out to your child the advantages of being on time (no rush, time to talk with friends before school starts, no arguing with you).

Impose a Penalty for Disobedience
If your preschool child won't get himself ready (which is the easy way to do things), show him that you can make him do it the hard way with physical assistance (page 128). Without nagging or yelling, put his clothes on him, wash his face, and offer him food. If he won't eat in a reasonable amount of time, let him go hungry (learning the hard way, page 101).

Tips

- Give your child a ten-minute warning before you "help" him get ready.
- Play a "beat the clock" game by challenging him to get dressed before the fifteen-minute kitchen timer goes off.

Schoolwork

Cathy does not like to do homework. She likes to play with her friends after school. She likes to play with her video games after supper. And she likes to watch TV after her bath. There is just no time in her day for homework. "Every day I have to physically sit her down, open her book put a pencil in her hand, and order her to do her work," says Cathy's dad. "In two minutes, she'll have to go to the bathroom, and then she'll need a drink, and then she'll be hungry. I feel like a security guard. If I don't sit right next to her and make her finish what her teacher says she has to do, it just doesn't get done."

REMEDY

Set a Limit
"You must do all your homework immediately after supper. It must be finished before you can watch evening TV."

Emphasize the Positive

- Praise his efforts to do his homework.
- Show interest in his school assignments.

Impose a Penalty for Disobedience
If your child does not follow the homework rule, give him a brief scolding (page 119) and do not let him watch TV at all that evening (loss of a privilege, page 118).

Tips

- Work with your child's teacher. Ask for a list of daily assignments. Ask for a daily progress report. Ask him or her to support the limits you have set.
- If your child has a lot of work to do, set the kitchen timer to signal a break time. Then set it again to remind him when it's time to get back to work.
- Give him a comfortable, quiet place to do his homework.

Sharing

Tara ran around her playroom in a panic. She was clutching as many toys as she could hold to her chest and screaming, "Mine!" Her cousin was trying to play, but Tara would scream again every time she touched a toy. "You must share your toys," Tara's mother scolded. "Now put all those toys down, and let your cousin play with whatever she wants. She's your guest and you must let her play with your things." Tara put down the toys, ran to the corner of the room, and cried.

REMEDY

Set a Limit

"You may hold one toy in your hands, and you may keep it for yourself. If you put it down, anyone may play with it."

Emphasize the Positive

- Praise your child when he shares.
- Set a good example by sharing your things with friends and relatives. (If a neighbor asks to borrow your lawn mower, don't grumble and complain about the imposition.)

Impose a Penalty for Disobedience

- Use time-out (page 122) if your child refuses to let another child play with a toy that he is not using.
- Remove the problem toy from the play area (loss of a privilege, page 118).

Tips

- Sharing is a learned developmental task that is not usually attained until a child is three or four years old, so don't expect one or two-year-olds to share willingly. Show them how, encourage them to do it, but then stand close by to play referee when the fights start.

- Put away your child's favorite toy when friends visit so he does not have to "give away" something very special.
- When two children insist on playing with one toy, try giving the toy to one child and set the timer so it will signal when it's time to give it to his friend. Then set the timer again to signal when it's time to give the toy back.

Sibling Fights

Blake and Jay were at it again:
"Cut it out!"
"You started it."
"I did not!"
"Yes you did."
This kind of arguing, wrestling, pushing, and yelling went on all day long at the Cannon house. "I try to let them work it out themselves," says the boy's mom, "but sometimes the fights get so rough that I really feel I have to do something. Usually I just add the sound of my own yelling to the noise and they keep right on fighting."

REMEDY

Set a Limit
"You two have to play without disturbing me with your noise, and without name-calling or hitting each other."

Emphasize the Positive

- Praise your children whenever they play nicely together.
- Show them alternate ways to settle their disputes, such as talking it out, drawing straws to see who goes first, using a timer to signal when it's time to trade toys, or playing in separate rooms for a while.

Impose a Penalty for Disobedience

- Use a time-out (page 122) for both children when you do not witness who started the fighting. Don't argue, nag, or try to solve the dispute. Calm them both down by separating them in time-out chairs placed in different rooms.
- If you see one child bother another child, punish the instigator with a penalty appropriate to his action. If, for example, you see Blake bite Jay, look up "biting" in this chapter and follow the suggested discipline procedure (page 166).

Tips

- You can sometimes prevent sibling fights that are caused by a need for space if you allow each child to have his own toys and his own section of the room.
- You can sometimes prevent sibling fights that are caused by a need for your attention by giving each child his own piece of quality time each week (page 25).
- Sibling fights are a normal occurrence in every household where these are more than one child. Try to ignore normal bickering but intervene quickly and consistently when the children become verbally or physically abusive.

Spitting

Six-year-old Wendy spits. She spits on other children when she's angry, and she also spits on the ground just for the fun of it. "I don't know where she picked up this disgusting habit," says her mom. "No one in our family spits, and I certainly don't want Wendy to do it either."

REMEDY

Set a Limit
"People in this family do not spit. You are not to spit anymore because it offends other people and it shows very bad manners."

Emphasize the Positive

- Model good manners by making sure no one in your family spits.
- Praise your child whenever he has an opportunity to spit but doesn't.

Impose a Penalty for Disobedience

- As with other aggressive acts, impose an immediate time-out (page 122) when your child spits on other people.
- If your child is spitting on the ground, it is probably done to get your attention and make you angry. In this case, ignore the behavior (ignoring, page 97).

Tips
If your child insists he must spit because he has a lot of saliva in his mouth, tell him to use the sink where no one can see him. If the spitting continues, you should ask your pediatrician if your child has a physical problem.

Stealing

Three-year-old Todd stood next to his mother at the check-out counter with his hands shoved deep into his coat pockets. After his mom bought the milk and bread that she needed, they got back into the car and headed for home. "I glanced into the rear-view mirror," says Todd's mom, "and saw Todd sitting in the back seat chomping on a wad of gum. I knew he didn't have any gum before we went into the store, and I knew I didn't buy him any. I pulled the car over to the side of the road and sat there stunned. It hurt to even think that I was about to accuse my son of stealing."

Set a Limit
"You cannot take things that don't belong to you because it's wrong, it's against the law, and it makes people angry."

Emphasize the Positive

- Explain the difference between borrowing and stealing. Young children don't automatically know that stealing is wrong.
- Teach your child to ask for things when he wants them.
- Be sure to set a good example. Don't take towels from a motel and supplies from work and then give your child a lecture on the evils of stealing.
- Praise your child when he asks you to buy a pack of gum that he previously might have stolen. Reward him by buying it.
- Place a high value on personal honesty and respect for the property of others.

Impose a Penalty for Disobedience

- Tell your child, "If you take things that are not yours, you'll have to go back to return it and apologize (right the wrong, page 115). If the stolen item cannot be returned (like chewed gum for instance), tell your child, "You must pay for what you've taken." He can do this either with allowance money or by doing a few chores to work off the debt.
- Give your child a brief scolding (page 119). Don't nag or scream; just state that stealing is wrong, explain why, and offer an alternative way of obtaining the things he wants (like asking for them, saving allowance and gift money, doing chores).

Tips

- Don't get hysterical the first time your child takes something that doesn't belong to him. He is not yet a hardened "thief," so don't call him one.
- Don't ask your child to self-incriminate: "Where did you get that?" Confront him with the fact: "I know you took that from Jimmy's house." Then calmly use one of the penalties suggested above.

Sometimes children "steal" because they honestly don't know better. The discipline steps listed above are appropriate ways to teach a child that taking other people's property is wrong. However, some children steal for more complex psychological and social reasons. If your child habitually steals despite the fact that he knows it's wrong, he may need professional counseling to overcome this problem, which may be psychological in origin rather than a form of simple noncompliance.

Tattling

"Mommy, Joan is not going right to sleep; she's reading a book."

"Daddy, Freddy is playing in the dirt and getting all dirty."

"Teacher, Rhonda is fighting with Irene."

Mandy is a tattletale. She is quick to report the misdeeds of her sister and friends every chance she gets. "I hate you!" screams her sister. "You always tell Mommy everything I do when it's none of your business."

"It's true," says her mom. "Mandy feels this need to tell adults what other children are doing wrong. It's almost like she thinks this makes her look better."

REMEDY

Set a Limit

"Don't tell me what your sister and your friends are doing wrong, unless they are a danger to themselves or others, because it makes them dislike you."

Emphasize the Positive

- Praise your child for telling you something good about his friends.
- Set a good example by avoiding gossip in your own conversations.

Impose a Penalty for Disobedience

- Ignore the intent of the tattling (which is to get the other child in trouble) with a curt "I'm sorry the two of you aren't getting along," or "that's too bad."
- Use a brief scolding to remind your child that you disapprove of tattling (page 192).

Tips

Consider the reason for your child's tattling. Most often it's done to enhance his position in your eyes. To avoid this, don't thank the tattler and punish the child who has been tattled on. When you set a limit on tattling, be sure to explain to your child that he *should* tell you when someone is doing something that is dangerous. Give examples about the kinds of things that are okay to "tell." For example, lighting matches, throwing rocks at another child, putting a rope around someone's neck, drinking alcohol, or taking drugs are legitimate causes for "telling." It's important that your child knows he can tell you when the actions of siblings or friends are dangerous to themselves or others without being scolded for tattling.

Teasing

Since teasing a sibling or friend is similar in intent to name-calling, use the same discipline strategies suggested in "Sibling Fights," page 188, and "Name-calling," page 184.

Temper Tantrums

Two-year-old Bradley rules his home with his screaming, foot-stomping displays of anger. Whenever his parents say no, Bradley throws a temper tantrum, and he'll keep it up until his parents give in to his demands. "I can't stand it when Bradley throws himself down on the floor and starts kicking and crying," says his dad. "I know I shouldn't, but after five minutes of that I'll give him anything he wants."

REMEDY

Set Limits

"You will not get what you want by throwing a temper tantrum because that is not how people in this house act." (Be sure to explain exactly what constitutes a temper tantrum: screaming and kicking and crying, for example.)

Emphasize the Positive

- Teach your child how to handle anger and frustration through your own example. Instead of flying into a rage when you spill chocolate milk on your new white sweater, for example, tell your child how angry it makes you feel and then show him how you'll take care of the garment so the stain won't set.
- Watch for frustrating situations that will probably set off a temper tantrum. When you see his building of blocks fall down for the second time, for example, offer him help before his frustration shows itself in a tantrum.
- Praise your child when he is able to follow your directions, seek your attention, or handle a frustrating situation without having a temper tantrum.

Impose a Penalty for Disobedience

- When your child has a temper tantrum for the purpose of getting your attention or getting what he wants, ignore it (ignoring, page 97).
- If your child is having a tantrum because you've asked him to do something he doesn't want to do (like clean up his toys), let him have the tantrum, ignore it, and when he finishes be sure to make him do the task he's crying about.
- If your child's tantrum escalates into a show of aggression or destruction, don't ignore it. Throwing things, biting, hitting, or destroying things should never be ignored. At that point put him in the time-out chair until he calms down.
- If your child throws a temper tantrum in a public place, it's not a good idea to ignore it because other people have a right to a peaceful environment. Find an out-of-the-way place (your car, a stairway, a park bench) where you can carry your screaming child to and impose a time-out until he calms down (the time-out place, page 123).

Tips

- Look for patterns in the occurrence of your child's tantrums. If they happen every day just before dinner, or late in the evening, for example, perhaps hunger or fatigue could be their trigger.
- Expect temper tantrums from children eighteen-months to three years old. Yelling at your child and using excessive forms of punishment will not eliminate their occurrence. (See Appendix A, page 204, for developmental information.) Instead, teach your child that anger is normal and help him practice other ways of expressing it. But remember, until your child becomes better able to verbally express himself and has more self-control, temper tantrums are to be expected.

- Don't try to talk your child out of a temper tantrum. It won't work.
- When your child has a temper tantrum, don't label him a "bad boy." Disapprove of the behavior, not of the child himself.

Throwing Things

Six-year-old Alison likes to throw things. When her dad asks someone to pass the dinner rolls, she throws them to him. When her mom asks her to clean up her toys, she throws them across the room into the toy chest. And very often, for no apparent reason, she'll pick up a household object and throw it across the room. "I think she's developed a bad habit and doesn't even realize that she's throwing things that could break or hurt someone," sighs her mom.

REMEDY

Set a Limit

"Don't throw things, because they may break, or they may break something in the house, or they may hit someone and hurt them."

Emphasize the Positive

- Praise your child when he resists the impulse to throw and places an item where it belongs.
- Set a good example by not tossing things, like toys or garden tools, into their proper place.
- Give your child things that he can throw, like balls, bean bags, and balloons.

Impose a Penalty for Disobedience

- If a toy breaks when your child throws it, don't fix or replace it (learning the hard way, page 101).

- If a toy is thrown but does not break, take it away and put it in the Saturday Box (loss of a possession, page 118).
- If your child throws something and breaks a household object (like a vase or picture frame), make your child clean up the mess and replace it with allowance money or money earned by doing some chores (right the wrong, page 115).

Tips

If your child throws things in anger or at other people, it is an act of aggression like hitting or biting. In addition to the consequences listed above, it should be handled with an immediate time-out.

Touching Dangerous Household Objects

Two-year-old Amy is curious. She wants to feel, touch, and explore everything, especially the things she isn't supposed to. "Everytime I turn around," her mom says, "Amy is into something dangerous. She loves the electrical sockets, and she pulls off the safety caps I've put on them. She keeps trying to stick her fingers into the cassette player and turn all the control knobs on the stereo. And I'm getting really worried that she'll get burned when she touches the oven or the radiators."

REMEDY

Set a Limit

"You can not touch the electrical outlets, because you can get hurt." (Set a separate limit for each item. "Stay away from dangerous things" is too vague.)

Emphasize the Positive

- Praise your child when he approaches a dangerous object but listens to your warning and turns away.

- If possible, don't tease your child by letting him watch you use the object you want him to stay away from (the stereo and electrical outlets, for example).
- Distract your child away from dangerous objects by offering him safe ones.

Impose a Penalty for Disobedience

When your child touches a dangerous object, give him an immediate brief scolding (page 119) and physically remove him from the area. Do this consistently whenever he approaches the dangerous object.

Tips

- You can teach a young child to stay way from dangerous items by following the guidelines listed above, but you confuse him if you have too many "no" items in your house. Move the stereo, put away the plants, and restructure your home so your child can explore without getting hurt or destroying your things (page 48).
- Most of the touching problem is the result of normal curiosity. Help your child grow and develop by encouraging the exploration of special drawers and closets that you fill with safe utensils, pots, and other interesting "adult" things.

Whining

Seven-year-old Tony is a whiner. When he's bored, tired, or frustrated, he whines to his parents with a nasal intonation that can unnerve them in thirty seconds:

"I have nothing to do."

"I'm thirsty."

"I don't want to watch this show."

"My shirt is dirty."

"I don't want to go to school."

And on, and on, and on.

Set a Limit
"I cannot understand you when you talk like that. If you want me to answer you, you'll have to talk in a normal tone of voice."

Emphasize the Positive

- Praise your child when he asks nicely for something.
- Demonstrate the correct way to ask for something, such as: "Mommy, may I have a glass of water, please?"
- Set a good example by cutting back on your own bouts of complaining.

Impose a Penalty for Disobedience

- Ignore the whining (page 97).
- If you can't ignore the sound of whining, put your child in the time-out chair where you can't hear him (page 123).
- Give your child a brief scolding (page 119).

Tips

- When you tell your child, "Don't whine," be sure to give him an example of what you mean. Imitate the sound so he can hear exactly what you disapprove of.
- Some children resort to whining when they are overtired. You may be able to control the whining problem by making sure your child has enough sleep. If fatigue is the cause, the above penalties will do little to stop the behavior.
- If your child can take a joke, you may be able to break his whining habit with humorous imitation. Announce that for the next ten minutes, everyone in

your house will practice becoming "whiners." Carry on all conversations in a whining tone (and hope that no one calls to talk to you on the phone). When your child hears how silly he sounds, he may give up his whine. (Be sure to laugh at the behavior, not the child.)

OTHER COMMON CHILDHOOD PROBLEMS

The discipline problems listed above can all be controlled with the three-step program of discipline. The following six problems are also quite common, but they're more complex in their causes and treatments and therefore require a more detailed discussion than is possible within the format of this book. If you need help handling the following childhood problems, you can find the information you need in a book called, *How to Help Children with Common Discipline Problems,* by Charles E. Schaefer, Ph.D., and Howard L. Millman. Ph.D. (Signet Books).

1. Persistent lying
2. Nail-biting
3. Overeating
4. Persistent stealing
5. Thumb-sucking
6. Undereating

If your child suffers from problems with toilet training or bedwetting, you might also want to read: *Toilet Training Without Tears,* by Charles E. Schaefer, Ph.D., with Theresa Foy DiGeronimo (Signet Books).

When a child persistently exhibits unacceptable behaviors without any regard for right or wrong, he may be suffering from deep-rooted psychological and/or emotional problems. It is quite normal for children to exercise their need for independence through noncompliance. But when this noncompliance becomes a persistent and automatic response with hostile intensity, then it becomes an abnormal action and in this case both the child and his parents need professional guidance. For example, the frequent and intense occurrence of lying, stealing, bullying, or showing cruelty to animals should be professionally addressed before it becomes a deep-seated psychological problem. You can call your state or county psychological association and ask for a referral to a psychologist who can help you with your specific concern, or you can call your local school psychologist and ask him or her for a referral to a family counseling psychologist or agency.

Afterword

Good discipline begins when parents set down a secure foundation for their family relationships. The three-step program of discipline presented in this book has given you the information and the skill you need to build that foundation and to use it as a base from which your child will learn self-discipline and self-esteem. In sum, this program explains how to:

1. Strengthen the bonds of your parent/child relationship through self-awareness, unconditional love, and honest communication.
2. Set limits that are reasonable, consistent, and enforceable.
3. Enforce limits with a variety of tactics that include rewards, penalties, and lack of attention to the undesirable behavior.

When parents do these three things consistently, they soon learn to promote good behavior by emphasizing positive actions, encouraging good intentions, and understanding and correcting mistakes—and all without ever ranting, raving, yelling, or resorting to physical punishment.

As you use and practice these parenting skills, always keep in mind that no one can use all these skills all the time because no one is a perfect parent. Pick out the discipline strategies that you're most comfortable with and use them with persistence. If one day you find yourself pulling out your hair in frustration and resorting to old habits like screaming or spanking, don't throw away the whole program and all your efforts up to that point. Simply wait until you're calm, reevaluate which discipline tactics you want to use, and start again. Eventually, when your children learn what you expect from them and how you will react to misbehavior, there will be little need for your emotional tirades, and if you should occasionally lose control, it won't permanently disrupt the behavior expectations you've established throughout the three-step program of discipline.

The goal of a good discipline program is to teach a child how to behave and at the same time to instill a sense of right and wrong that will guide his actions and foster a sense of self-control throughout his lifetime. *Teach Your Child to Behave* has given you a program of discipline that was created with this goal in mind. If you use it consistently with determination, you'll ensure that when your child walks away from you on his own, he'll be headed in the right direction.

Appendix A
Child Development

Children progress through fairly predictable stages during their first few years of life. Parents who know what to expect are better equipped to ignore and permit certain behaviors that might otherwise surprise and anger them. Parents who don't know about these stages are hesitant to alter their disciplinary strategies to accommodate their child's age because they see this as a form of giving in. They reason, "My son should learn how to walk around the house without knocking over my plants. If he runs, he'll have to be punished until he learns not to do it." This attitude doesn't take into account the relationship between a child's age and certain behaviors. The parents, for example, who refuse to put away their valuable glassware because they feel two-year-old Jimmy must learn to respect their belongings are not respecting Jimmy's lack of physical coordination and his underdeveloped sense of cause and effect. Most likely, the glassware will break, Jimmy will be punished, but no positive lesson will have been learned.

It is difficult for children consistently to obey rules that are not appropriate for their age. The information in this appendix will make it clear, for example, that:

- Two-year-old Jeff isn't being intentionally naughty when he refuses to share his toys. Most two-year-olds are struggling to gain a sense of "me" and "mine"; anything they get their hands on becomes "mine." They are most often incapable of sharing anything.

- Four-year-old Tammy isn't being intentionally naughty when she spills her milk. Most four-year-olds are easily distracted and move around in their seats a lot. This fact, combined with their unrefined coordination skills, very often make a full glass of milk an inevitable mess.
- Six-year-old Greg isn't being intentionally babyish when he begins to whine around dinnertime. Although he's too old for an afternoon nap, he still gets very tired later in the day. When this happens a 6-year-old will usually have trouble controlling his emotions.
- Eight-year-old Lauren is a latch-key child. She doesn't mean to ignore her mother's after-school instructions, but there are just too many of them for her to follow. Feeling overwhelmed, she does nothing.

Before you decide to discipline your child, stop to determine if the problem is caused by willful disobedience, or by your child's stage of development. You can do this by referring back to this guide, by talking with other parents who have children the same age, by reading books about the stages of child development, and by asking professional people (your pediatrician, a psychologist, or your child's teacher) if particular behaviors are appropriate for your child's age.

The stages of development as they are listed below are general comments on what most children do at certain ages. A child's emotional and intellectual growth, however, is not an exact science that can be pinpointed to a specific age, nor generalized to all children. Use the following information as a guideline to enhance your use of the three-step program of discipline. Do not use it to rate or evaluate your child.

BIRTH TO ONE YEAR

In this first year of life it is not appropriate to set or enforce limits because children at this age cannot understand the cause and effects of discipline. You cannot communicate to them the kind of logic that says, "If you obey this rule, you will be rewarded, but if you break this rule, you will be punished."

In the first year, preventive discipline strategies are the best way to control disturbing behaviors. Specific techniques are explained in Chapter Two, and include baby-proofing the house so your child has freedom to explore in a safe environment; distracting his attention from the things you don't want him to do (like ripping up your magazine); and ignoring the crying when his needs have been met. This is also a good time to lay the groundwork for future behavioral expectations by setting a good example through your own actions.

ONE-YEAR-OLDS

In this second year of life, children begin to follow simple directions like "no" and "come." They begin to learn that there are limits to what they can and cannot do. They generally do not have enough internal discipline nor long-term memory to follow household rules consistently, however. They need constant reminders and guidance as they learn, for the first time, that life has limits.

A one-year-old:

- Likes to play in the same room with other children, but will not usually interact with them.
- Can distinguish between "mine" and "yours," and begins to have appreciation of other people's property.
- Has intense curiosity that is not matched by an understanding of danger and so he will play with matches and be totally unaware of the danger.

- Is advancing in the verbal and motor skills that help him become more aware of himself as a person who can assert his own will. (This may result in temper tantrums.)
- Will push his physical ability to the limit (and sometimes beyond) by climbing, jumping, and falling.
- Loves cabinets, drawers, and boxes.
- Likes to fill containers and dump them. (Watch your wastebaskets!)
- Has a desire to use utensils (like spoons and forks) that exceeds his physical ability to do so.
- Will get himself into more things as he learns how to turn knobs and flick switches.
- May develop sleep problems.
- Is unpredictable in his eating habits. He will pick at food with his fingers, push it aside one day, and gobble it up on the next.
- May insist on self-feeding with a spoon. (Most of the spoon's contents will end up on the floor or in his lap.)
- Is learning to undress himself (and may do so at inopportune times).

Help your one-year-old learn how to behave by:

- Allowing him to practice things like self-feeding without worrying about the mess.
- Being available to guide and nurture.
- Encouraging his need to explore.
- Learning to live with a reasonable amount of mess.
- Expecting noisy play.
- Encouraging his struggle for independence from you.
- Permitting and ignoring childish behaviors that do not infringe on other's rights or endanger others or themselves.
- Reserving the word "no" for important matters that endanger his or others' safety.
- Continuing to baby-proof your house and using preventive discipline strategies (see Chapter Two).

TWO-YEAR-OLDS

The "terrible twos" can be a difficult time for you and your child. It is a time when children generally become argumentative and respond to most requests with an automatic no. Although this may drain your patience, it's important to remember that this negativism is a normal, healthy stage that helps children define themselves as human beings separate from their parents. It is a mistake to take a two-year-old's stubborn, obstinate attitude too seriously or punish him too severely for it. Save your objections for those few negative behaviors that endanger his or other's safety, and set and enforce reasonable and guiding limits. This will lay the foundation for teaching your child self-control.

A two-year-old:

- Has an improved ability to use and understand language.
- Can help dress and undress himself.
- Can learn how to wash himself.
- Can grasp the concept of "pretty soon" and "in a while."
- Can learn to put things where they belong.
- May be aggressive, self-centered, and demanding.
- Is bursting with energy.
- Is not wise or responsible, (*Super* baby-proof your home.)
- Will begin role-playing and imitating (feeding a doll, talking on the phone, sweeping the floor).
- Needs to manipulate and touch (will want to play in mud, dirt, and water).
- Will explore genitalia.
- Likes routines and will complain about changes.
- Wants to do things himself ("me do it") but is easily frustrated when is physically or mentally unable.
- Has flashes of temper and mood changes.
- Plays beside but not with children his age.
- Has difficulty sharing, waiting, taking turns, or giving in.

- Will try to drag out bedtime.
- Understands more words than he can speak.
- Can remember directions for only five minutes.
- Will begin to recognize danger and so may avoid playing with knives or in the street.
- Is rigid and inflexible. He wants things done a certain way and no other way.

Help your two-year-old learn how to behave by:

- Keeping rules simple and direct.
- Setting only a few limits that are important for safety reasons.
- Altering your home environment to accommodate his need to explore safely.
- Expecting spilled milk.
- Providing safe play outlets.
- Giving choices, such as saying "Do you want cereal or toast?" rather than "You must eat breakfast."
- Accepting sexual curiosity as normal.
- Having patience!

THREE-YEAR-OLDS

Phew! Your child is now less concerned with asserting his independence. Three-year-olds know they are separate from their parents and will spend a good part of their day trying to be like them in this "me, too" stage. As their desire to please their parents grows, it becomes easier to teach them how to behave.

A three-year-old:

- Will begin to listen to reason: "Clean up your toys so you won't trip over them."
- Has increased manual dexterity (can hold a crayon, cut with safety scissors, build with blocks).
- Will interact with other children.
- Likes to role-play policeman, fireman, cowboys, TV characters, and so on.

- Is less stubborn.
- Develops a desire to please adults.
- May have an imaginary friend.
- Loves to stretch the truth and tell "stories" (don't call them "lies" yet.)
- Still may prefer finger eating to spoons and forks.
- Has a strong drive to be "grown-up." Will imitate, mimic, and act out adult roles.
- May "borrow" an object without understanding that it must be returned.
- Can learn to dress and feed himself.
- Should be encouraged to ask for things rather than point for them.
- Will speak in short-phrase sentences.
- Will have trouble understanding "yesterday" and "tomorrow."
- Is beginning to understand that other people have feelings too and will show sympathy to a hurt friend.
- Can now express anger and frustration verbally rather than physically.
- Has a budding self-concept that is greatly affected by what others say about him. Statements like, "You're a bad boy," may be taken as absolute truth.
- Will begin to develop personal standards of right and wrong.
- Will listen to why a rule is important.
- May develop fears (of the dark, or abandonment, for instance.)
- Has little patience but can learn to wait his turn.
- Can take on some responsibility like hanging up his coat or putting away toys.
- Shows evidence of a conscience.
- May release insecurity and frustrations by whining and crying.

Help your three-year-old learn how to behave by:

- Expecting and ignoring grammatical mistakes in his speech.

- Arranging opportunities for him to play with others his age.
- Accepting imaginary friends into your family.
- Giving opportunities for your child to dress and feed himself.
- Fostering a sense of responsibility by assigning a daily chore.
- Being especially watchful of your own behavior; you will see it played back by your three-year-old.

FOUR-YEAR-OLDS

Your four-year-old is learning to fit into a world outside of his immediate family. As a sense of peer pressure develops, it becomes important for these children to be considered "one of the gang." They are beginning to feel a sense of concern for others and will defend the rights of their friends as the concept of fairness begins to take shape. At this age it is very important to explain the reasons *why* some behaviors are not acceptable.

A four-year-old:

Will seriously test the limits you set and may want to change them and make up new ones.
- Is starting to make sense of rules if they are explained.
- Will play tricks and loves adventures.
- Has a new interest in numbers.
- May be a bit rude, noisy, boastful, bossy, and rebellious.
- Can now do two things at once (color a picture and eat a snack).
- Will make up reasons for his behavior that will seem completely illogical to you. ("I couldn't come inside when you called because Tommy made me eat carrots.")
- Takes on the characteristics of the people he plays (the courage of a superhero, the bravery of a fireman, and so on.)
- May take something from a friend's house if he likes it without realizing that stealing is unacceptable.

- Likes to talk and listen. Communication is now fun rather than a task to be learned.
- Has improved memory skills. He can remember three directions at one time: "Finish your snack, put on your coat, and come outside."
- Can estimate how long a task will take.
- Has an understanding of "yesterday" and "tomorrow."
- Is learning the concepts of "a lot" and "a little."
- Is learning to handle his own emotions and will talk about uncomfortable situations.
- Will avoid aggressive actions when angered and will look for a compromise.
- Is starting to seek approval more from other children than from adults.
- Can play alone for more extended periods.
- Can recognize his own neighborhood.
- Starts projects but may not finish them.
- Quarrels fiercely and then forgets about it.
- Uses bathroom words (like, "pee-pee" and "poopey") in a silly way.
- Giggles a lot.
- Can grasp the concept of reward for good behavior and negative consequences for bad.

Help your four-year-old learn how to behave by:

- Giving your child some say in making the household rules.
- Asking him (in advance of trouble) to help establish the consequence for breaking rules.
- Letting your child go "along with the crowd" as long as their activities aren't harmful to anyone.

FIVE-YEAR-OLDS

When five-year-olds enter kindergarten, they often come to believe that they know everything there is to know about what's right and what's wrong. They will begin to lecture you about the evils of smoking. They will warn you to "say no to drugs." They will explain the rules of a game in great detail and squawk at the idea that rules can bend or be changed. Any attempts at cheating are quickly and harshly noted. This is also the age of the tattletale who wants everyone to know when someone else is not obeying the rules. Although he may argue about your rules, your five-year-old is fully ready to understand and follow the limits you set for him.

A five-year-old:

- Will talk excessively and comment on every move you make.
- Begins to gain awareness of time in the distant past and future. He may begin to question you about his birth and your childhood.
- Is unable to judge the time it takes to cross the street.
- Is able to love and care for animals.
- Is more able to obey commands, especially once he begins school.
- Will mix reality, imagination, and daydreams into oral stories.
- Has speech patterns that are now more clear and logical.
- Has a tendency to interrupt adult onversations with "something really important." This is most likely an attempt to keep your attention focused on him.
- Can and should do simple household chores.

Help your five-year-old learn how to behave by:

- Permitting some of his bossy, know-it-all attitude.
- Being firm in your enforcement of limits. This may become more difficult now that your child has the verbal ability and persistence of thought to try to talk you out of it.
- Realizing that the line between reality and fantasy is still often indistinguishable.
- Giving your child a sense of responsibility and self-esteem by assigning him chores that he can do with-

out your help and that he must do every day. Such chores include setting the table, emptying wastebaskets, putting his clothes in the hamper, feeding the dog, or sweeping the porch.

SIX- TO EIGHT-YEAR-OLDS

Children ages six through eight have developed an aura of worldliness. Their time at school and at friends' homes is time away from you and your influence. Now, the beliefs, values, and attitudes that you have instilled in them are being adjusted to fit those of their teachers, friends, and their friends' parents (which may sometimes clash with yours). These children need a little slack in the reins of discipline to allow them to question, test, and compare household rules, even though your decisions will usually prevail.

The six- to eight-year-old:

- May become quite industrious now that he is learning how to organize his work, set his mind to a task, and complete it.
- Will create a strong bond of friendship with a special pal.
- Will be very sensitive to peer pressure and so will try to model the behavior of others his age (even when that behavior is unacceptable to you).
- Knows his right from his left side.

Help your six- to eight-year-old learn how to behave by:

- Giving him some room to occasionally make decisions with which you may disagree (like hairstyle and clothing choices, for example).
- Letting him work with you to negotiate the household rules and determine the consequences for disobedience.
- Listening carefully to his arguments· and reasons, and bending when you can see his point. But make sure that he always knows you are in charge.

Appendix B
Suggested Reading

The following books each contain a variety of effective discipline techniques that may compliment the three-step program of discipline.

Bodenhamer, Gregory. *Back in Control.* Prentice-Hall, 1983.

Clark, Lynn. *SOS! Help for Parents.* Parents Press, 1985.

Ginnot, Hiam. *Between Parent and Child.* Macmillan, 1965.

Gordon, Thomas. *P.E.T.—Parent Effectiveness Training.* Peter H. Wyden, 1970.

Isaacs, Susan. *Who's in Control?* Putnam, 1986.

Nelson, Gerald, and Richard Lewak. *Who's The Boss?* Shambhala, 1984.

Schaefer, Charles. *How To Influence Children.* Van Nostrand Reinhold, 1982.

Wyckoff, Jerry, and Barbara Unell. *Discipline Without Shouting or Spanking.* Meadowbrook, 1984.

Index